Careers Counselling in Practice

First published in 1984, *Careers Counselling in Practice* is intended as a practical guide and a review of developments in careers work. It surveys careers counselling and guidance practice in schools, colleges and universities as well as work done outside the educational field by vocational guidance agencies. The book draws freely on examples of guidance practice and in particular makes mention of trends in American careers education and guidance. In reviewing transition agencies and services, it argues firmly for an educational rationale for careers work and counselling rather than a guidance model based on state employment agencies. This is an important reference work for career counsellors, educationists and policy makers.

Careers Counselling in Practice

Ben Ball

R Routledge
Taylor & Francis Group

First published in 1984
by The Falmer Press

This edition first published in 2024 by Routledge
4 Park Square, Milton Park, Abingdon, Oxon, OX14 4RN

and by Routledge
605 Third Avenue, New York, NY 10017

Routledge is an imprint of the Taylor & Francis Group, an informa business

Publisher's Note
The publisher has gone to great lengths to ensure the quality of this reprint but points
out that some imperfections in the original copies may be apparent.

Disclaimer
The publisher has made every effort to trace copyright holders and welcomes
correspondence from those they have been unable to contact.

A Library of Congress record exists under ISBN: 0905273699

ISBN: 978-1-032-94427-2 (hbk)
ISBN: 978-1-003-57068-4 (ebk)
ISBN: 978-1-032-94429-6 (pbk)

Book DOI 10.4324/9781003570684

Careers Counselling in Practice

Ben Ball

The Falmer Press

A member of the Taylor & Francis Group
London and Philadelphia

UK   The Falmer Press, Falmer House, Barcombe, Lewes, East Sussex, BN8 5DL

USA   The Falmer Press, Taylor & Francis Inc., 242 Cherry Street, Philadelphia, PA 19106-1906

Copyright © Ben Ball 1984

First published in 1984

Library of Congress Cataloging in Publication Data

Ball, Ben.
   Careers counselling in practice.

   Bibliography: p.
   Includes indexes.
   1. Vocational guidance.   I. Title.
HF5381.B24   1984   331.7′02   84-1616
ISBN 0-905273-69-9
ISBN 0-905273-70-2 (pbk.)

Typeset in 11/13 Caledonia by
Imago Publishing Ltd, Thame, Oxon

Jacket design by Leonard Williams

Printed in Great Britain by Taylor & Francis (Printers) Ltd, Basingstoke

Contents

To Linda, William and Sophie

List of Tables and Figures

Chapter 1

Chapter 2

Chapter 3

Chapter 4

Chapter 5

Chapter 6

Preface

The significant changes in patterns of employment and the dramatic rise in the rates of unemployment, particularly amongst young people over the last decade, have presented a serious set of challenges to careers practitioners. This is most particularly so of careers advisers and careers advisory services who have traditionally seen job placement as the central focus for their work and who see their work primarily as helping young people to find work in a contracting labour market. The spectre of coping with large numbers of clients who have been unemployed for long periods, who face little prospect of finding a job, must challenge much of what goes on under the heading of careers guidance. Additionally the very notion of paid employment being available to all is now under question, particularly in the absence of any political will to stimulate economic activity to generate jobs. Conventional notions of what constitutes work are now up for review, particularly the notion that work is inevitably linked to paid employment. Many of the changes in the employment structure are of course attributable to the introduction of microprocessor technology, the reduced demand for labour and the consequential shedding of thousands of jobs in the manufacturing sector, a process which seems set to have a major effect on the service sector of the economy (Jenkins and Sherman, 1979). Many of the changes in the nature of work and the structure of employment are summarized by Hopson and Scally (1981) and Showler and Sinfield (1981). The size and scope of these changes and their implications, face careers practitioners, who seek to keep a grasp on what's happening in the labour market, with a major conceptual challenge! The very term 'career' suggesting, as it does to some, a linear career pattern characterized by increasing development and specialization in one occupation, poses problems for its use. Careers practitioners and careers services may therefore be hard put to explain their role to clients whose experience is either that there is no work or else that unplanned and enforced changes of job and occupation do not constitute a career in the previously accepted sense.

Changes in the employment structure have also brought about major changes in the provision of education and training opportunities, particularly for school leavers. The Manpower Services Commission's Youth Training Scheme with its guarantee of a training place for *all* 16-year-olds after leaving school represents a major shift in the responsibility for the vocational preparation and training of young workers, with employers being given generous financial allowances for training large numbers of young people. Unlike the Youth Opportunity Programme, the employers themselves will be able to recruit directly to schemes. The local authority careers services may therefore have a diminished role in placing young people and while all Youth Training Schemes have to provide key elements such as training, induction, work experience, guidance and counselling, and assessment, it remains to be seen what the implications of this will be for careers services and individual careers advisers. The government's New Technical and Vocational and Vocational Education Initiative (NTVEI), a pilot scheme for reintroducing technical and vocational education in schools, may well have considerable implications for school-based careers teachers and careers coordinators. The complexity, then, of systems, admissions, and entry requirements to the various routes in education and training increases the difficulty of the task for careers teachers and careers advisers of knowing precisely at any given time the full range of opportunities available to any particular client. At best, they are able to keep abreast of provision in their own local geographical area and in their own community. The same is, of course, true on a national level, for careers advisers working in further and higher education, with many more of their clients entering courses of further training in the face of a contracting job market.

Most of the changes documented so far are concerned with the structural change, of which individual careers practitioners and helping professionals have to make sense, before they can be effective in helping their clients. No mention has so far been made of the increased difficulty of finding appropriate ways of responding to and helping clients whose development has been blocked or denied because of their difficulties in finding and keeping work. The emotional strain of being in a role which is intended to help clients find work at a time when jobs are decreasing in number will inevitably result in work stress for those employed in this area of work. Many careers advisers and counsellors will doubtless find themselves in a catch-22, in which they are helping professionals paid to help clients, find and retain and develop in work, but are unable to fulfil clients expectations, because jobs do not exist. Cast in a supportive role, and confronted with the reality of a contracting employment market, careers practitioners are therefore faced with a number of dilemmas. How far can they encourage their clients to be ever more competitive in a protracted search for decreasing number of jobs and, as Kirton (1983) documents, how far should they try to influence clients to be more realistic in their job preference and accept whatever work is available? How active can they be in encouraging clients to think of alternative approaches to finding and creating work?

In the face of the changes described above this book represents an attempt to document some of the ways in which careers practitioners can respond in the situation in which they find themselves, and its aim is to review and evaluate changes in current practice in careers education and counselling. To this extent it may have something to say both to existing practitioners as well as to those newly involved in training. As the title suggests, it is concerned largely with practical issues and approaches in a variety of educational settings. One of the major assumptions made, which some may find difficult to share, is that the problems faced by careers advisers and counsellors are broadly the same no matter what the educational setting — school, college of further education or university — and apply irrespective of the age or type of the client. The book therefore draws freely from examples of practice from all sectors of the education system. Chapter 1 is concerned with the theoretical assumptions which underpin much of a careers practitioner's work. Chapter 2 is concerned with developments in careers education in a variety of educational settings. Chapter 3 provides an appraisal of the nature of the helping interview and practical guidelines on how to carry out careers counselling interviews. Chapter 4 reviews the current aids to career decision-making and the role of careers information, occupational interest guides and the role of computer-based guidance programmes. Chapter 5 reviews the aims of the transition services and helping agencies in this country and Chapter 6, the role of the community in careers guidance programmes. The final chapter is in the form of a directory of resource materials that can be used for careers education.

Finally, perhaps a word or two of definition is required concerning the use of the terms 'guidance' and 'counselling' in this book. The term 'guidance' is used to denote the sum total of an educational institution's provision in preparing its pupils and students for working life. The author shares the view of Milner (1974) and Daws (1976) that guidance is a global term and it embraces the entire range of careers activities (careers programmes and work experience schemes and placement activities).

Careers 'counselling', on the other hand, can be defined as the process of helping and enabling people in their career development, of which the central focus is the helping interview. To this extent it can be seen as the major focus for the careers practitioner's work. One of the main arguments put forward in the following pages is that the term 'careers counselling' more accurately describes and therefore supplants what some authorities still describe as the vocational guidance interview.

In writing this book, I have been grateful for the support of a number of colleagues, in particular Linda Buckham for her continued encouragement.

Chapter 1

Career Development

Career development can be seen as the process of individual growth, learning and development in relation to work. It is characterized by the accumulation of experience, career decisions and adjustments made throughout an individual's working life. Work, it is frequently acknowledged, provides both a major source of personal identity and a medium through which the total personality can express itself. In the context of paid employment, the process of career development is commonly characterized by a number of different stages and statuses, from apprentice or trainee to qualified professional or skilled worker through to 'old hand' or trainer. As Super (1957) points out, however, the process of career or vocational development begins well before the entry to work,

> Like other aspects of development, vocational development may be conceived of as beginning early in life, and as proceeding along a curve until late in life. Thus the four-year-old who plays carpenter or storekeeper is in a very early stage of vocational development, and the septuagenarian who no longer teaches or does research but still attends scientific meetings or writes his professional autobiography is in a very late stage of vocational development.

It also needs stressing that career development is not solely concerned with describing stages and accomplishments within paid employment, but embraces work in any context, as well as the life style it affords. Hansen (1977) sees the concept of career development as

> ... a lifelong process of self-clarification, as a consequence of positions one holds in a lifetime, as the various choices and decisions one makes to implement a life style, and the ways work and leisure fit in with the kind of person one perceives herself or himself to be. This definition assumes that consideration of work

is intimately related to family roles and patterns and to matters of career-marriage conflict and commitment. Drawing from career development theorists and developmental psychology, the definition includes such career management tasks as developing positive self-concepts, gaining control over one's life, and maximizing vocational possibilities; such goals as awareness of self, awareness of preferred life styles, formulation of tentative career goals, clarification of the decision process, obtaining employability skills, interpersonal skills, a sense of planfulness, and commitment with tentativeness within a changing world.

Career development is therefore concerned with the relationship between the individual and work in its broadest sense, whether this is work in the home or paid employment, whether it involves a set career pattern, is characterized by stable employment in the same job for twenty years, or by frequent job change or redundancy.

This broad and all encompassing definition of career development needs to be carefully distinguished from those which concern a narrower perspective of employee career development in organizations. Schein (1980) and Hall (1976) both describe attempts by large employing organizations to foster the personal and career development of their workforce and to achieve some synthesis of individual and organizational needs by structured career development programmes. Career development in this narrower and more specific sense of staff and organizational development falls outside the scope of the present chapter.

Theoretical Approaches

A review of the literature of career development reveals that researchers have taken a number of different approaches to provide some understanding of the nature of the career development process. Studies of occupational choice and placement, career maturity and career patterns have all contributed to the sum total of presently available research data and are comprehensively summarized by Watts *et al.* (1981). By way of summary, it would seem that theoretical explanations of career development can be grouped and differentiated in a number of ways. Super (1981) distinguishes between matching models, whether derived from the psychology of individual differences or sociological and structural explanations and developmental models with their emphasis on life stages and decision-making approaches. Law (1981) provides a further dimension by drawing a distinction between those theories which assume that occupational choice is an automatic process and those that seek explanations in terms of individual autonomy. Hall (1976) distinguishes between matching theories, which describe what kinds of people enter what occupations, based on some measure of compatability and the chosen occupation, and process theories which describe the way individuals gradually arrive at choice of occupation, taking into account individual choices and decisions as organizational selection. From a purely sociological standpoint, Speakman (1980) draws a clear distinction between 'objective' explanations of occupational choice in terms of economic conditions and labour market considerations and 'subjective' explanations which centre on individual aspirations and orientations. Arguably, however, from the point of view of careers practitioners, the most striking distinction is that between theories of occupational choice and career development which are derived from psychological explanations and those which arrive from sociological standpoints. In this country, the debate has raged over the last ten years between adherents of the opportunity model of Roberts (1977) and those of psychologically-based explanations of the career choice process (Daws, 1977). Briefly summarized, the debate concerns the extent to which occupational choice can be understood by psychological explanations in terms of individual choice and ambition or by sociological explanations which tend to be concerned with structural factors which limit or shape ambitions and aspirations. The salient points of this debate are summarized in Figure 1.1.

Figure 1.1. *A Comparison of the Guidance Implications of Ambition and Opportunity Structure Models*

Model	Explanation	Process	Guidance Implications
Individual ambition	Psychology	Choice	Decision-making and autonomy is fostered
Structure/ opportunity	Sociology	Allocation	Traditional guidance intervention is questioned

As Speakman (1980) points out, the central question is how far individuals are free to make informed choices which fulfil needs are self-concepts and how far choices are effectively limited by boundaries established by family, educational system and occupational structure. If one accepts an explanation of the entry into work in terms of an opportunity structure model, one is, according to Roberts (1977), acknowledging that 'guidance merely lubricates more basic process of occupational selection'. It is therefore the aim of the present chapter to examine both psychological and sociological perspectives on career development and to consider the implications for practitioners involved in careers education and counselling.

Talent Matching Approaches

Parsons' *Choosing a Vocation* (1909) is generally acknowledged to be the first statement of the aims of careers guidance and laid the foundation for the development of trait and factor approaches to guidance work. According to Parsons:

> In a wise choice there are three broad factors:
> (1) a clear understanding of yourself, your attitudes, abilities, interests, ambitions, resources, limitations and their causes:
> (2) A knowledge of the requirements and conditions of success, advantages and the disadvantages, compensations, oppor- tunities, and the prospects in different lines of work:
> (3) True reasoning of the relations of these two groups of factors.

The concept of 'true reasoning' to which Parsons refers is generally thought to have been a matching of an individual to a particular job on the basis of rational judgment, an activity to be carried out by the careers guidance practitioner with the help of testing and the use of adequate occupational information. The overall approach suggested a matching of individual talents to particular kinds of work. The applica- tion and development of Parsons' ideas in the careers guidance field owed a great deal to the rapid developments that took place in applied psychology in the inter-war period. Psychometric measures of intelli- gence and aptitude were used widely by American authorities in the selection of personnel for the armed services in both world wars and test results were seen as reliable predictors of performance in various tasks.

In World War I, for example, group intelligence tests were used by the American army for officer selection, assignment of personnel to different types of service and to reject or discharge those who were unfit for military service. In the immediate post-war period group tests for intelligence were then widely used in educational and industrial settings, and as Anastasi (1976) points out, the testing boom of the twenties did a good deal to retard the progress of psychological testing.

In World War II specialized test batteries were used by the American and British armed services in the selection of radio operators, pilots and other technical/specialist functions, many of which are still currently in use.

It is not surprising that the careers guidance practitioners of the time began to employ the self same techniques that were used in selection, for it now seemed theoretically and, indeed, technically possible to match, almost exactly, the patterns of ability or 'traits' of individual workers with those 'factors' of performance required in a particular job. Careers guidance could therefore be seen to be an empirical task, based firmly on the psychology of individual differences and carried out with the latest available psychometric tools.

Since that time the optimism surrounding the use of measures of intelligence and aptitude in careers guidance work has been dissipated and a number of studies, including that by Thorndike and Hagen (1959), have challenged the notion that test data can adequately predict occupational success and performance. Other factors it seems need to be taken into account when predicting occupational success and suitability. In particular, the assumption underlying the talent-matching approaches that there is one suitable job for a given individual has been challenged by the developmental theorists Ginzberg *et al.* (1951) and Super (1957).

Talent matching and trait and factor approaches still have their adherents and the work of most, if not all, of the private vocational guidance agencies is based on the assumption that psychological testing can be used to predict which are likely to be suitable career opportunities for clients. In reasserting the traditional perspective of differential psychology and summarily dismissing developmental perspectives, Kline (1975) asserts 'the essence of vocational guidance, fitting a man to a job, lies in accurate assessment of people and in the accurate description of jobs ... theories of vocational development do not seem of great importance especially to the practitioner.'

Whereas most trait and factor approaches to career development place considerable emphasis on the matching of people's abilities to particular jobs, Holland's theory is concerned with the part played by and influence of personality in occupational choice. Simply stated, Holland's theory concerns the way individuals with a given set of personality characteristics are likely to find themselves in work environments which are consonant with their personality. Conventional people, Holland would argue, have to find congenial work in conventional work environments, if the opportunity arises.

Holland (1966) postulates that:

1   there are six broad categories of personality: Realistic, Investigative, Artistic, Social, Enterprising and Conventional [a full description of each personality type is provided in a later chapter];
2   that there are six types of environment each populated by individuals of the corresponding personality type;
3   people search for environments that will let them exercise their skills and abilities, express their attitudes and values and take on agreeable problems and rules;
4   a person's behaviour is determined by an interaction between his personality and the characteristics of his environment.

Four additional concepts characterize Holland's theory:

a   consistency — the degree to which the different personality types co-exist happily with each other;
b   differentiation — the extent to which one individual can be ascribed to any one category;
c   congruence — the degree of goodness of fit between individual and environment;
d   calculus — which describes, according to Holland,

> 'the relationships within and between types or environments can be ordered according to a hexagonal model in which the distances between the types or environments are inversely proportional to the theoretical relationships between them.

According to Holland's model, therefore, it is likely that some personality types will be closely related, for example, Enterprising and Social, but those on opposite ends of the hexagonal model are the least alike, for example, Artistic and Conventional (see Figure 1.2). Furthermore, in choosing work, individuals with a given personality profile are likely to make for work environments which allow them to express their personality type.

In support of his theory, Holland has developed two measures of occupational interest, the Vocational Preference Inventory and the Self Directed Search, both of which have been widely used by vocational counsellors in the United States. As Clarke (1980b) points out, Holland's work has attracted a tremendous amount of international research work, much of which is broadly supportive of his ideas. Sadly, little of this research has been carried out in this country.

Figure 1.2.   *Hexagonal Model Showing the Relationship between Personality Types*

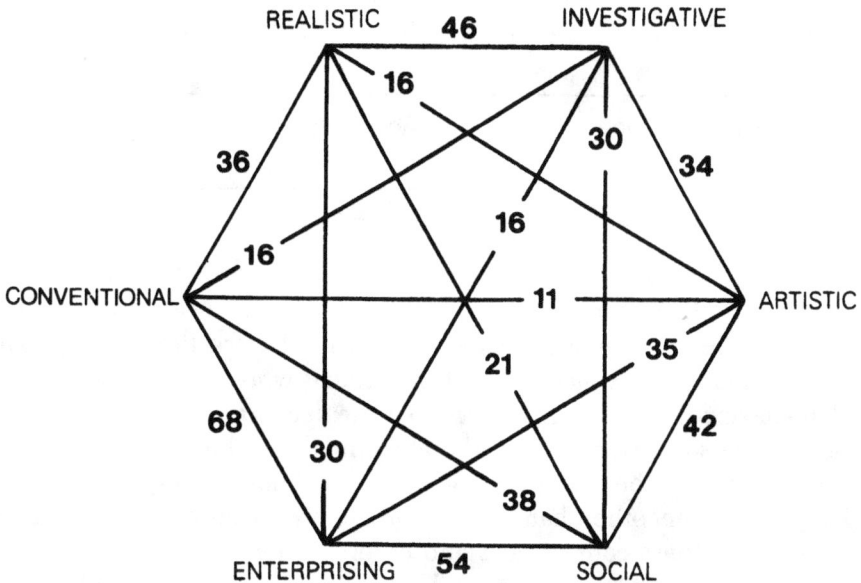

Source: John L. Holland (1971) *A Counselors Guide to the Self Directed Search*, reproduced by special permission of the publisher, Consulting Psychologists Press, Inc., Palo Alto, CA 94306.

According to Weinrach (1979) however, Holland's theory is not without its critics. Like other talent matching theories based on occupational interests it is charged with being too static and simplistic a model with which to describe all the factors influencing occupational choice. In particular, Weinrach argues the

> theory does not explain sufficiently how people come to fall in one personality type rather than another or point to the learning process of socialisation and other factors which makes one person 'realistic' and another largely 'social'.

A theoretical perspective which concerns early influences on personality rather than a personality typology is provided by Roe (1956). Roe stresses the importance of early childhood experience and psychodynamic factors in determining occupational choice. In reviewing the range of parental behaviours in childrearing, Roe distinguishes six styles of behaviours:

| 1 Over-protection | Emotional concentration on the child |
| 2 Over-demanding | |

| 1 Emotional rejection | Avoidance of the child |
| 2 Neglect | |

| 1 Casual acceptance | Acceptance of the child |
| 2 Loving acceptance | |

Source: A. Roe (1956) *Psychology of Occupations.*

These six styles, Roe argues, will determine whether in their future development people will be person or non-person oriented, which in turn will be a major influence on the type of work they choose. The assumption in Roe's model is that individuals whose early experience is characterized by emotional rejection or neglect are likely in adult life to be non-person oriented and therefore in their choice of work enter occupations in the fields of science or technology. Person oriented people, on the other hand, are more likely to enter occupations in service, business contact, arts and entertainment.

As Hall (1976) points out, subsequent research has provided little support for Roe's theory, presumably because of the methodological problems of obtaining biographical data about early childhood experience and relating these to career choice. If person or non-person orientation is a significant factor in predicting occupational choice, Hall argues, then one needs to ask why the influence of this variable has not been examined, rather than try to explore the range of childhood experiences.

Developmental Models

The psychological approaches to career development described so far are based on the concept of individual differences — that people who have different needs, aptitudes and interests will choose work to suit those needs by making one career decision. However, the theoretical framework which has had the most impact on careers counselling practice in this country and the United States is that which sees work entry and occupational choice as part of a developmental process, rather than a single event which acknowledges that individuals and jobs change in relationship to each other over time. Two early works, Ginzberg *et al.'s Occupational Choice* (1951) and Supers' *The Psychology of Careers* (1957), have done much to influence the practice of careers guidance and counselling in the last thirty years.

Drawing on their own research evidence and perspectives derived from developmental psychology, Ginzberg *et al.* (1951) put forward the notion that occupational choice has a process rather than being a single life event, 'an individual never reaches the ultimate decision at a single moment in time, but through a series of decisions over a period of many years, the cumulative impact is the determining factor.' The process, lasting from childhood to late adolescence and young adulthood, is characterized by three stages, Fantasy, Tentative and Realistic (see Figure 1.3). After the Fantasy period in childhood, in which work roles are often assumed in play, the Tentative stage can be divided into four stages: *interest*, in which individuals clarify their likes and dislikes; the *capacity* stage of testing abilities against aspirations; the *value* stage at which perceptions of occupational styles emerge; and the *transition* stage in mid-teens which is concerned with preparation for a career decision. The Realistic period is again differentiated into *exploration*, *crystallization*, and *specification*; substages all concerned with the process of synthesizing ideas about career options and coming to a decision. The process as a whole can be seen as one in which the

Figure 1.3. The Stages of Career Development

Ginzberg		Super	
Fantasy	Childhood (up to age 11)	Growth	(birth−14)
Tentative	Early Adolescence (ages 11−17)	Exploration	(ages 15−24)
		Crystallization	(ages 14−18)
Substages;		Specification	(ages 18−21)
Interest		Implementation	(ages 21−24)
Capacity			
Value		Establishment	(ages 25−44)
Transition			
		Stablization	(ages 24−35)
Realistic	Adolescence and Adulthood (age 17 onwards)	Consolidation	(age 35+)
		Maintenance	(ages 45−64)
Substages;		Decline	(ages 65+)
Exploration			
Crystallization			
Specification			

Source: E. Ginzberg, *et al.* (1951) *Occupational Choice*, New York, Columbia University Press; D.E. Super (1957) *The Psychology of Careers*, New York, Harper and Row.

9

adolescent gains increasing self-awareness in relation to an awareness of his or her immediate environment, and the external realities of the work place. Ginzberg made a number of other postulates about the nature of career development and decision, firstly that the process is largely irreversible, since each career decision and subsequent experience will have an impact on future decisions, secondly that because choice involves a synthesis of an individual's ideas and preferences and what is in reality possible, career decision-making is to some extent a matter of compromise.

These original ideas have been subject to some modifications since they were first published, largely because the research on which they were based was carried out mainly with a middle-class, college educated sample. Subsequent research with low-income groups and the under-educated led Ginzberg to different conclusions.

In a later article Ginzberg (1972) revised his theoretical statement concerning the decision-making process and its elements of compromise and irreversibility. The process of decision-making, he later argued, was not confined to the period of adolescence but was a life-long process of change and adjustment. While still maintaining that educational and occupational decisions had a cumulative impact on later career be-haviour, he sought to give the idea of irreversibility less prominence, by pointing out that often young people's career behaviour is characterized by wanting to keep all their options open as long as possible (which in an oblique way almost seems to confirm young adults' perception of the irreversible nature of career decisions!). For 'compromise' Ginzberg later substituted the word 'optimize', presumably because of its more positive and purposeful connotations.

Finally, Ginzberg's reformulated theory states that: 'occupational choice is a lifelong process of decision making in which the individual seeks to find the optimal fit between his career preparation and goals and the realities of the world of work.'

Super's theoretical perspective is avowedly developmental and owes much to Ginzberg's earlier work. It is, however, the perspective which has had the greatest influence on the practice of careers counselling in both Britain and the United States. Many of Super's ideas are expressed in his twelve propositions listed in Figure 1.4 (Super, 1981); these provide a comprehensive statement about the theoretical assumptions implicit in his work. They admit that career development is characterized by a loosely defined matching process between indi-viduals and jobs, but, more importantly, that the process of occupational choice which is characterized by a series of life stages of career development, is, according to Super, one of compromise and adjust-

Figure 1.4   Super's Twelve Propositions Concerning the Nature of Career Development.

Proposition 1	People differ in their abilities, interests and personalities.
Proposition 2	They are qualified, by virtue of these characteristics, each for a number of occupations.
Proposition 3	Each of these occupations requires a characteristic pattern of abilities, interests and personality traits, though with tolerances wide enough to allow both some variety of occupations for each individual and some variety of individuals in each occupation.
Proposition 4	Vocational preferences and competencies, the situations in which people live and work, and hence their self-concepts, change with time and experience (although self-concepts are generally fairly stable from late adolescence until late maturity), making choice and adjustment a continuous process.
Proposition 5	This process may be summed up in a series of life stages characterized as those of Growth, Exploration, Establishment, Maintenance and Decline, and these stages may in turn be subdivided into (a) the Fantasy, Tentative and Realistic phases of the Exploratory stage, and (b) the Trial and Stable phases of the Establishment stage.
Proposition 6	The nature of the career pattern (that is, the occupational level attained and the sequence, frequency, and duration of trial and stable jobs) is determined by the individual's parental socio-economic level, mental ability, and personality characteristics, and by the opportunities to which he is exposed.
Proposition 7	Development through the life stages can be guided, partly by facilitating the process of maturation of abilities and interests, and partly by aiding in reality testing and in the development of the self-concept.
Proposition 8	The process of vocational development is essentially that of developing and implementing a self-concept: it is a compromise process in which the self-concept is a product of the interaction of inherited aptitudes, neural and endocrine make-up, opportunity to play various roles, and evaluations of the extent to which the results of role playing meet with the approval of superiors and fellows.
Proposition 9	The process of compromise between individual and social factors, between self-concept and reality, is one of role playing, whether the role is played in fantasy, in the counselling interview, or in real-life activities such as school classes, clubs, part-time work, and entry jobs.
Proposition 10	Work satisfactions and life satisfactions depend upon the extent to which the individual finds adequate outlets for his abilities, interests, personality traits, and values; they depend upon his establishment in a type of work, a work situation, and a way of life in which he can play the kind of role which his growth and exploratory experiences have led him to consider congenial and appropriate.
Proposition 11	The degree of satisfaction the individual attains from his or her work is proportionate to the degree to which he or she has been able to implement self-concepts.
Proposition 12	Work and occupation provide a focus for personality organization for most men and many women, although for some people this focus is peripheral, incidental, or even non-existent, and other foci such as social activities and the home are central.

Source: D.E. Super, 'Approaches to Occupational Choice and Career Development', in A.G. Watts, *et al.* (1981) *Career Development in Britain*, CRAC Hobsons Press. Reproduced by permission of Hobsons Press (Cambridge) Ltd., publishers of all CRAC materials.

ment, and primarily concerned with implementing a self-concept.

This latter idea is perhaps the cornerstone of much of Super's early work (1951; 1957). Simply stated, Super (1957) proposed that in starting work each individual is defining or elaborating their idea of themselves, 'the choice of an occupation is one of the points in life at which a young person is called upon to state rather explicitly his concept of himself, to say definitely "I am this or that kind of person".' The notion that in starting work or changing career we are at the same time testing ourselves against the reality of the work place and synthesizing our ideas about ourselves and our futures has been readily accepted into careers guidance practice. As Kidd (1981) observes, much of present careers guidance and counselling practice is concerned with fostering self-awareness and the development of the client's self-concept. While American research evidence has so far supported Super's theory of self-concept implementation, there is little British research evidence on which to draw to support or deny this aspect of occupational choice.

It is, however, Super's theoretical formulation of career choice as part of a life-long process of development that has attracted most interest amongst career practitioners. Building on Ginzberg's work and that of Buhler, Super *et al*. (1957) delineated five vocational life stages of Growth (Birth–14), Exploration (age 15–24), Establishment (age 25–44), Maintenance (age 45–64) and Decline (age 65 onwards), which are summarized in Figure 1.3. The *Growth stage* is characterized by identification with key figures in family and school and an increasing awareness of interests and abilities. It contains the substages of Fantasy, Interests and Capacity. The *Exploration stage* is characterized by increasing exploration of self in relation to work, when *Tentative* choices are made and implemented in mid-teens in preparation for the *Transition* stage of work entry and professional training. The *Trial stage* is concerned with adjustment and commitment to a particular field of work. The *Establishment stage* (age 25–44), as the name suggests, is the period during which an individual begins to feel estabished in a particular field and can be separated into two substages: trial (age 25–30) and stabilization (age 31–44). During the *Maintenance stage* (age 45–64) little new ground is often made in career development. The *Decline* (age 65 onwards) stage, coinciding with retirement from work, is seen as a time of deceleration, but with the chance to take on new roles and activities.

Having put forward the idea of career development as a life-long process, it was logical that Super should be led the question the nature of vocational maturity and how this could be achieved.

Evidence from Super's longitudinal study of some 200 boys, the Career Pattern Study, suggested that not all people experience a gradual development or crystallization of their ideas as their careers progress. Rather, Super found, one could determine different styles of career behaviour from long-term study. Before the age of 25, many of those in the survey exhibited 'floundering' behaviour, while at the age of 25 eighty per cent of subjects were seen to have stabilized in their career, which lends some credibility to his developmental life stage model (see Figure 1.3). Several other longitudinal studies of career development led to the design of measures to appraise vocational maturity. Super's own questionnaire, 'the Career Development Inventory', was an attempt to measure clients' occupational knowledge, consistency and realism of occupational preferences as well as knowledge of decision-making processes. As Kidd (1981) observes, the research effort which has gone into the assessment of vocational maturity in the United States has been of some considerable size and scope. Kidd, however, remains sceptical about the ready acceptance of these measures in a British context, primarily because of lack of statistical evidence of their validity; indeed, she doubts the usefulness of the concept of career maturity in careers guidance practice.

Sociological Perspectives

As we have already seen, sociological perspectives on work entry and entry and career development tend to describe a process of allocation of individuals in the workforce rather than acknowledge the idea of choice and ambition having an influence on an individual's life chances. The influence of family background, neighbourhood, schooling and peer group will, it is argued, have an impact on a person's choice of occupation and later career development.

In an important study of British school leavers entering work, Maizels (1970) found that parents had a major influence on the kind of work entered by their children and concluded that 'the vocational aspirations of children were thus influenced through the medium of personal relationships, developed and maintained over time.' Several studies have reached the same conclusions, Carter (1972) and Ashton and Field (1976) showing the link between the socio-economic status of parents and the work attitudes and aspirations of adolescents.

In a penetrating study of working-class boys and their transition from school to work, Willis (1977) was able to distinguish two distinct cultural groupings, which each had its own ways of anticipating life after school. The conformist group or 'ear-oles' accepted schooling and the need for paper qualifications. The non-conformist 'lads', on the other hand, rejected the aims of schooling and prepared themselves for well paid manual work. The cultural norms of these groups, Willis contends, are a major determinant of the kind of work entered after school. 'So far as the "lads" are concerned, all jobs are basically the same.' Arguing against the emphasis of individualism in the process of careers guidance and counselling, he asserts that 'the whole ideology and language of developmental psychology with its centrality of the individual and the meaningful choices open to him is a distortion of what's happening at a cultural level.'

In their study of the transition of young people into work, Ashton and Field (1976) were able to identify three distinct class-based groups, each characterized by different career behaviour. The 'career-less' (corresponding to Willis' 'lads') from working-class backgrounds tend to enter unskilled employment. Those from skilled working-class background enjoyed *short-term careers*, having been through apprenticeship or other training schemes. The notion of *extended career* was reserved for those from middle-class backgrounds who aspired to managerial job functions. Once again background and social milieu were shown to be useful predictors of the kinds of work entered by young people. In addition, Ashton and Field argue, there is a complex interrelationship of social class background and educational experience which is likely to determine occupational choice.

They conclude, 'it became clear that for most young people there is a basic continuity in their experience at home, at school and at work such that the kinds of beliefs they acquire about themselves and the perspectives they develop about the world at home and in the school are continually verified in their experience of work'. According to their model, the level at which young people enter the labour market is therefore largely determined by class background and educational experience.

None of the foregoing studies seeks to invalidate the role of careers guidance and counselling services in the transition of young people from school to work, simply to point to the impact of sociological determinants on occupational choice. The work of Roberts, however, raises particular challenges for careers practitioners and helping agencies. Roberts (1968, 1977, 1981) argues that the opportunity structure, rather than occupational choice, is the principal determinant of how people enter different kinds of work, that work entry and career development is determined more by opportunity than by choice. He remains critical of the way careers officers, in particular, have accepted developmental theories of career development; indeed, Roberts' early work was an attempt to find evidence for some of the postulates of Ginzberg and Super. In attempting to find evidence for the developmentalists' life/stage approach, Roberts (1968) tested three separate hypotheses:

that young workers' ambitions would be more consistent with their jobs as their careers develop;
job satisfaction gradually increases as careers develop;
occupational mobility declines as careers progress.

Perhaps, not surprisingly, Roberts found no clear evidence to support his hypotheses and concluded that amongst British school leavers 'occupational choice is frequently not the determinant of career behaviour'.

The evidence and arguments used by Roberts are common to many of the sociological perspectives on occupational choice and work entry. Occupational opportunities are structured by school or educational attainment and by home and family background. If, as research has shown, many young workers find work through family contacts, then the kind of work is going to be similar in terms of social status and proximity to that already undertaken by parents and family. Different groups of young workers, therefore, are going to be exposed to different opportunity structures. In his analysis, Roberts goes one step further than many sociological approaches, by asserting that ambition and aspirations are themselves determined by the economic and social structure. In other words, in this process of allocation, rather than choice, the kind of work we do is determined more by structural forces than by our own motivation and ambition.

It is for careers officers and careers teachers that Roberts' research has most critical challenge. By arguing that opportunities are structurally defined and the allocation of workers heavily determined by family influence, educational and occupational selection, Roberts is also arguing that careers guidance intervention, however well meaning, is of marginal value. Careers workers, Roberts argues, simply 'orient young people towards jobs they are structurally obliged to enter'. Like many researchers, however, it seems as though Roberts is assuming that careers practitioners claim a more powerful and directive influence than careers teachers or careers officers would ever dare to claim. Many careers practitioners would be happy to admit that one of their major roles was helping young workers to adjust to work, as much as it was to help them choose between work alternatives. To this extent many careers practitioners are happy to accept or collude with the structural forces which Roberts claims are operating and in practice are quite happy to channel the exaggerated aspirations of young adolescents towards more realistic options. Roberts seems to be wishing for careers workers an influence which in practice they do not enjoy, largely because of his assumptions that careers work is a talent matching and guidance process concerned with helping clients find work which is entirely commensurate with their wishes, rather than, as it often is, a process of helping clients find some limited satisfaction from the alternatives which face them.

Roberts is not without his critics; his major challenger in debate on behalf of the careers guidance and counselling movement has been Daws (1977; 1981). In particular, Daws (1981) argues that the opportunity structure model only partly explains the process of work entry and sees no reason why sociological and psychological explanations cannot be used simultaneously to explain aspects of vocational behaviour.

Daws' main argument is that the process of socialization is essentially a conservative force and that while there may be considerable pressures on young people to follow occupations related to those of their parents, the role of careers education programmes and counselling intervention is to raise clients' awareness of the range of opportunities available.

Secondly, Daws argues, increased participation in education and increasing social mobility have done much to blur the distinctions and divisions between social groups and their identities; he cites research evidence to show increasing rates of intergenerational mobility between classes. Young people entering the labour market, Daws argues, are therefore less likely to be influenced by parents and cultural background in choosing occupations, the more they are exposed to educational processes.

Daws' final criticism of Roberts relates to the impact of his ideas on everyday counselling and guidance practice. In setting up a structuralist theory, which denies the importance of choice and the helping agencies concerned with helping clients choose, Roberts has, Daws argues, undermined the enthusiasm of careers officers and careers teachers in carrying out their work. They should continue, however, to find evidence of the psychological variables which are at work in vocational behaviour, particularly in the transition of young people into work.

Much of the literature and research into the question of occupational choice and career development has, it seems, centred on the competing claims of occupational and developmental psychology, on the one hand, and the sociology of work entry, on the other. There is no reason, of course, why the theoretical perspectives and constructions of psychology necessarily exclude those of sociology and vice versa and it may be helpful to view the perspectives outlined earlier in this chapter as complementary rather than competing. In commenting on the need for an all-embracing theory of entry into employment, Daws (1977) states:

> ... Explanations derived entirely from one discipline will be inadequate. Furthermore, to demonstrate the importance of anticipatory socialisation does not preclude individual reflection and choice. The former defines the context within which the latter occur. What we do not know with any precision is the relative weightings of these processes in deciding the occupational experience of school leavers, particularly their relation to such variables as social class, ethnic group, sex, intelligence, educational qualifications, and age of commitment to an occupational choice.

One early theoretical approach which attempted to provide a model which accounted for sociological, psychological and economic variables is provided by Blau *et al.* (1956). The model proposed by Blau and his colleagues is outlined in Figure 1.5 and it suggests a complex interplay of psychological attributes, socialization and socio-economic structure. The immediate determinants of individual choice, the authors claim, are the occupational information clients possess, the qualifications they hold, their 'social characteristics' and value orientations, and these are matched against the determinants of selection and recruitment — job vacancies, skills and attributes required and employment conditions. Like Super and Ginzberg, Blau and his associates stress that career choice is not characterized by a single decision, but is revised repeatedly throughout one's working life.

Blau's model has such face validity that it is surprising that it has not attracted more research attention. As Hall (1976) points out, researchers have concentrated either on the factors influencing individual choice or on those concerning recruitment and selection processes. The interplay between these two processes has not been the subject of further investigation, presumably because of the methodological difficulties involved in examining such a complex interaction of forces and influences. The original thrust of the Blau model has not been examined empirically and the relative weightings of the different factors described by Daws and their influences on occupational choice and career development are still to be determined.

Having reviewed some of the more important contributions to career development theory, it may be useful for us to summarize the

Figure 1.5.   *The Blau et al. Model of Occupational Choice*

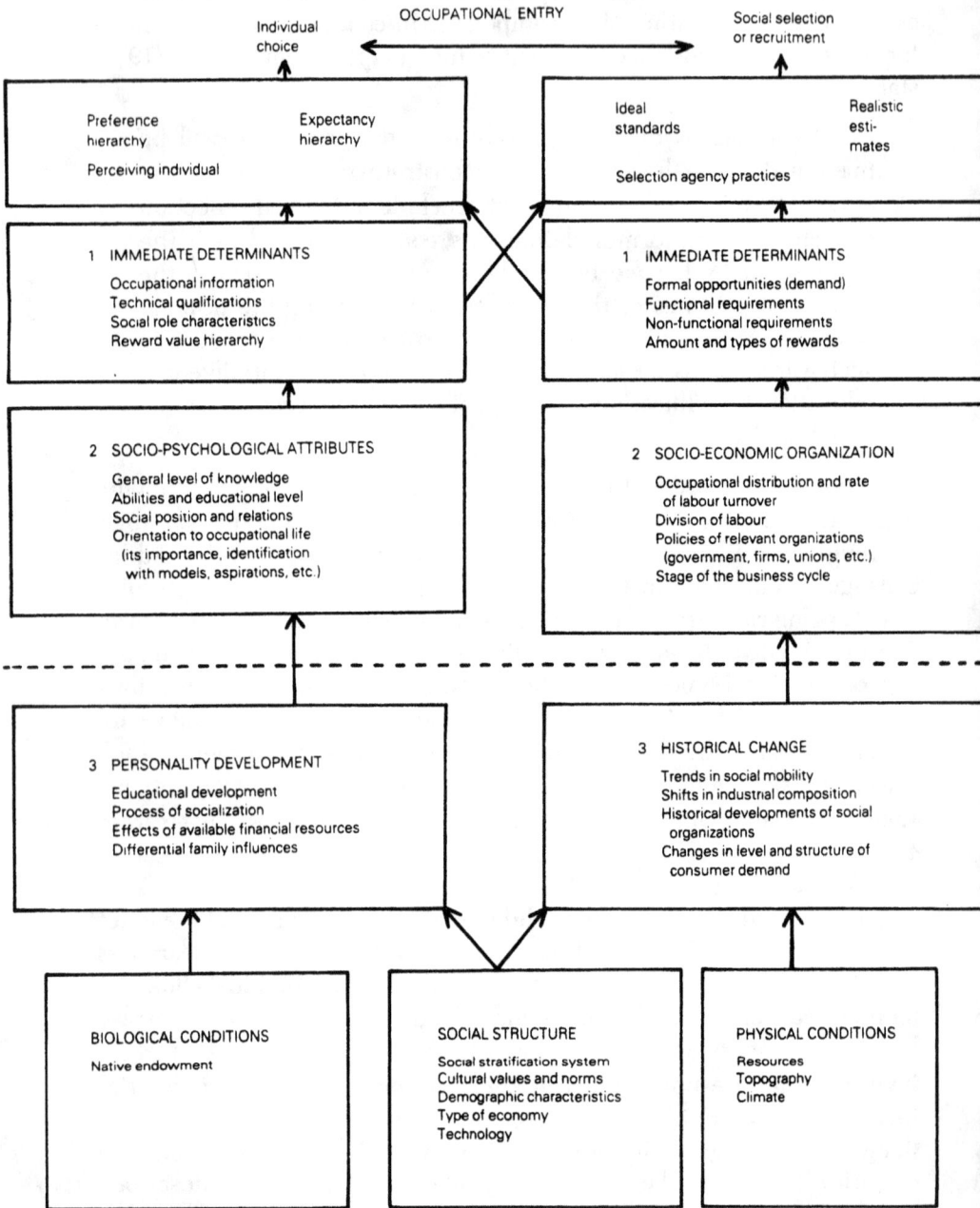

OCCUPATIONAL ENTRY

Individual choice

Social selection or recruitment

Preference hierarchy

Expectancy hierarchy

Perceiving individual

Ideal standards

Realistic estimates

Selection agency practices

1   IMMEDIATE DETERMINANTS

Occupational information
Technical qualifications
Social role characteristics
Reward value hierarchy

1   IMMEDIATE DETERMINANTS

Formal opportunities (demand)
Functional requirements
Non-functional requirements
Amount and types of rewards

2   SOCIO-PSYCHOLOGICAL ATTRIBUTES

General level of knowledge
Abilities and educational level
Social position and relations
Orientation to occupational life
  (its importance, identification
  with models, aspirations, etc.)

2   SOCIO-ECONOMIC ORGANIZATION

Occupational distribution and rate
  of labour turnover
Division of labour
Policies of relevant organizations
  (government, firms, unions, etc.)
Stage of the business cycle

3   PERSONALITY DEVELOPMENT

Educational development
Process of socialization
Effects of available financial resources
Differential family influences

3   HISTORICAL CHANGE

Trends in social mobility
Shifts in industrial composition
Historical developments of social
  organizations
Changes in level and structure of
  consumer demand

BIOLOGICAL CONDITIONS

Native endowment

SOCIAL STRUCTURE

Social stratification system
Cultural values and norms
Demographic characteristics
Type of economy
Technology

PHYSICAL CONDITIONS

Resources
Topography
Climate

Source: Reprinted, with permission, from Peter M. Blau *et al.*, 'Occupational Choice: A Conceptual Framework', *Industrial and Labor Relations Review*, 9, 4 (July 1956), p. 534. © 1956 by Cornell University. All rights reserved.

various perspectives and point to the implications for careers practitioners. Whether practice follows theory or vice versa, theoretical assumptions described in this chapter underpin many of the initiatives being taken in careers counselling and careers education and in one sense the remainder of this book is clearly concerned with the way in which careers practice relates underlying theoretical assumptions.

1 *Career Choice and Development As a Process*

There seems to be considerable agreement amongst both sociological and psychological perspectives that occupational choice is not characterized by a once and for all decision, but that careers choices and decisions undergo continual review during a life span. In reviewing a range of sociological perspectives on occupational choice, Sofer (1974) concludes:

> Our contributors accept and elaborate the viewpoint of the classical studies described that occupational choices and occupational decisions are probably best regarded as largely continual processes in that they are often the result of interaction over a protracted period between aspiration, preference, self-discovery, influence, opportunity and experience.

On this issue, therefore, there would seem to be a general acknowledgement that career decision-making is not characterized by a point-in-time event. This has particular implications for those who are concerned with the practice of vocational guidance based on talent matching approaches and is discussed in more detail in a later chapter.

From a practitioner's point of view, it helps to explain why some clients are readier to face work entry than others and why job change and adjustment problems are inevitably going to occur during the first years of real experience of work. It suggests that in counselling clients or before planning careers programmes, careers practitioners need to ask the question: 'At what stage are these clients in their career development?'

2 *The Effect of Class on Occupational Choice: 'As Far As the "Lads" Are Concerned, All Jobs Are the Same'*

Research indicates that home background, in particular social class, has a strong influence on the *level* of occupational choice, and both psychological and sociological perspectives on career development acknowledge this. The relationship between field or type of work and family background is less clearly defined, although several studies of undergraduates have shown that working-class students are far more likely to enter teaching than those from middle-class homes (Kelsall, *et al.* 1972). The effect of class and family in choice perhaps helps to explain why extremely able students from working-class backgrounds choose not to enter higher education when they have perfectly accept-able A-level grades. It helps to explain why some racial/cultural groups aspire to particular kinds of professional training and why some client groups 'switch off' from careers lessons, because they see 'careers' as something for middle-class students only. Finally, it implies that careers practitioners need to be able to ask of their clients: 'How are your family background and the expectations of your parents going to effect your choice of work?

3 *Career Advancement and Career Patterns*

The notion of a career as a life-time commitment to one job, charact-erized by steady advancement and promotion is challenged by a con-siderable amount of research evidence. As Watts (1981) suggests, the vertical model of career development is inadequate in explaining the process of career development of much of the working population and it seems reasonable to assume that with an increasing labour force and decreasing availability of paid employment that career development is going to be characterized in future more by lateral and horizontal career changes than by the vertical model which has always been assumed.

Proponents of the opportunity structure model of career develop-ment have always been able to discount the myth of the upward career spiral. As Roberts (1981) observes, 'there is no way in which everyone can climb to the summit of the occupational structure.'

4 *Cultural Influences on Career Development*

Our culture still retains in its folklore the concept that any person can become whatever he wishes if only he is willing to make the effort (Ginzberg, 1951)

It is evident that most of the theoretical perspectives that stress the importance of ambition and choice are American in origin and that in this country most of the theory and research on the question of occupational choice has emanated from academic sociology. As Watts and Herr (1975) point out, it is impossible to divorce theory and practice in careers counselling from wider cultural perspectives. It helps to explain why career education in the USA means something different from careers education in British educational settings and why counselling has not established itself in this country as it has in American education. It implies that practitioners have to be clear about the cultural perspectives they bring to their work and need to ask of themselves: 'How are the assumptions that underpin my work related to wider cultural values?

5 *The Impact of Unemployment*

Most of the research and resulting theoretical perspectives of career development presented in this chapter was carried out during a post-war period of economic prosperity and growth, with governments committed to notions of 'full employment'. As Ginzberg (1951) himself confirmed, 'Our findings and evaluations might have been entirely different in a period of mass unemployment or substantial underemployment, such as existed in the 1930s.' With unemployment now reaching the levels of the 1930s, it leads one to question the applicability of the results of previous research to the present problems experienced by young adults in finding work. Certainly, current employment conditions seem to lend tacit support to the opportunity structure model of Roberts (1977), since without employment, how can there be career development in the sense we have traditionally known it?

If one accepts the scenarios depicted by Jenkins and Sherman (1979) about the nature of the post-industrial society, it seems clear, that careers counsellors will have to concern themselves with careers work in the broadest sense of that term, which includes paid employment, unpaid work, and leisure, and permanent, full-time employment is likely to decrease in significance. Careers practitioners will have to ask how far they can concern themselves with the totality of an individual client's life experience, rather than focus primarily on paid employment.

6 *Allocation or Choice?*

There seems some agreement amongst the theoretical perspectives described earlier that career development is characterized by a complex resolution of different influences, the effects of socialization, parental influence and expectations, as well as the expression of individual needs and personality, but that it has proved difficult to quantity the differential effects of any of these influences.

The view put forward by Roberts (1981) that personal values are socially determined and dependent on opportunity structures is useful for careers practitioners' understanding of a client's frame of reference and in providing an awareness of client groups with special needs, for example, the unemployed. However, it fails to explain satisfactorily how a client's values and aspirations can be translated into the search for rewarding work. Robert's analysis cannot provide complete answers to the question which all careers practitioners have at the back of their minds: 'How and why do different individuals undertake different kinds of work?'

It seems reasonable to assume therefore that work entry and career decisions are influenced by psychological as well as sociological determinants. Which, however, is the major determinant has still to be established empirically, and whatever Roberts suggests about the influence of the opportunity structure it seems clear that individuals are rational and *purposive* in their career behaviour (Box and Ford, 1967) and that individual motivation cannot be discounted as a factor in career development (Law and Ward, 1981). Whatever the exact nature of post-industrial society and the kind of economy it assumes, individuals will still be left with choices and decisions about the kinds of lives they lead and the nature of the work they wish to do.

Chapter 2

Careers Education

Those not directly involved in careers counselling and guidance provision are often surprised by the concept of careers education; that it is not simply concerned with 'teaching people about jobs', but encompasses a far broader set of aims concerned with helping students learn to anticipate and prepare for their future working lives. Part of this surprise is no doubt due to the fact that in practice careers education can take many different forms and that the term 'careers education' is still a relatively new one. It is however an increasingly important area of educational concern and the aim of this chapter is to give some definition to the concept of careers education and to describe the forms it can take in various educational settings and with different client groups. A useful starting point is to contrast the development of careers education in this country with the origins of careers education in the USA. As Watts and Herr (1975) point out, careers education in American educational settings has been seen as a curriculum reform, an ideological standpoint, which attempts to influence the entire curriculum and make it more relevant to adult life and the world of employment. It has therefore become an educational movement which seeks to infuse the school and college curriculum to make it more relevant to the needs of community and industry. According to Isaacson (1977), it is as much concerned with developing positive attitudes to work on the part of the nation's youth and showing how they can contribute to the nation's economy as it is with facilitating individual student choices. This approach is summarized by Hoyt (1972):

> Career education should become part of the student's curriculum from the moment he enters school. It relates reading, writing and arithmetic to the varied way in which adults live and earn a living. As the student progresses through school, the skills, knowledges, and above all, the attitudes necessary for work success are stressed. This stress is phased into every

subject for every student, not just in separate classes designed for those who are 'going to work'.

To achieve a truly career-oriented education will require major changes in the way we now conduct the business of education. It will require new structure and innovations, a new relationship between that which is now academic, general, and vocational in education and a greater interaction among home, school and community.

The model of careers education as an activity undertaken by home, school and community is also characteristic of American approaches. According to Tolbert (1980), there are four models for careers education: a school-based model which centres on a career and life planning curriculum, with specific objectives for each year group often throughout the secondary years of schooling; an experienced-based model, very similar to British work experience schemes, but on a far more lengthy and structured basis taking into account individual learning needs of the students taking part; a home-based model for adults using radio, television and other media; and a residential-based model. For Hoyt (1975), American careers education programmes which are experience-based succeed because of their 'action orientation' and involve students in practical activities in the wider community outside school.

In marked contrast, British careers education seeks to promote a more realistic and narrowly focused set of objectives. In this country careers education has come to be a supplement to the school or college curriculum concerned explicitly with career decision-making and the transition from school to work. In this sense it is arguably more student centred than American career education approaches. According to Watts and Herr, in careers education in this country

> ... the main objective has been to help the student acquire concepts, skills and information which will help him (her) to formulate and implement the career decisions that immediately face him (her), though some attention has been paid to the fact that they will also help him (her) when facing subsequent career decisions — indeed it is this notion of equipping students with enduring resources for career development, which is one of the main justifications for an educational approach to careers guidance.

In practice, therefore, careers education in this country has come to be a curriculum component concerned with increasing students' knowledge of the range of opportunities available, helping them clarify their own sense of their abilities, interests and values, fostering decision-making skills. In analyzing the concerns of a number of school-based careers education programmes, Law and Watts (1977) have suggested a four-fold classification of careers education curriculum objectives comprising

1 the development of self-awareness;
2 increasing opportunity awareness;
3 the fostering of decision-making skills and preparation for career entry;
4 encouraging transition learning.

This has become the most widely adopted definition of careers education in this country and has been used to describe the development of careers education activity in a wide range of educational settings. As this chapter attempts to show, careers education can be seen to be developing along parallel lines in secondary, further and higher education settings.

Decision Learning

Being asked to articulate or state a personal preference may be quite a new task for many adolescents who are more likely to see decision-making as something done to them, rather than something they do for themselves. However, fostering career decision-making skills is a central feature of the careers education process since most of us acknowledge that we may be faced with the question 'What am I going to do' at any number of stages in our career development. The aims of encouraging decision learning are to encourage clients to:

a become more aware of the kinds of decision-making styles and strategies they habitually employ; and
b to improve the way they set about decision tasks.

It is to do with increasing clients' awareness and developing skills and behaviours. Typically, career decision-making programmes have a number of common components concerned with identifying and evaluating alternatives and the clarification of personal values and interests. In teaching decision-making in schools and colleges, it is often useful to use as illustrations consumer decisions or those drawn from interpersonal relationships. American career decision programmes in particular stress the need for logical and systematic approaches to the decision-making process and this theme is covered in greater detail in a later chapter.

Transition Learning

Transition learning is concerned with helping clients prepare for some future stage in their career development, to anticipate the changes that are likely to occur in their lives and the demands of a new situation and life style. For the average school leaver, this could take the form of lesson time devoted to personal finance and budgeting or how to build effective work relationships. For a student group in further education or higher education it could take the form of informal discussion about the process of starting work and coping with work routines and the demands of paid employment. In most careers education programmes it commonly takes the form of an examination of work rituals, the use of leisure time, the role of management and unions and the kinds of adjustments working life demands. In terms of timing in a class, activities transition learning is usually left to the last year of school and undertaken in the period immediately prior to departure. In many ways, the final year undergraduate, seeking work for the first time will be faced with exactly the same transitional process as school leavers and may lose his identity as 'student' and replace it with that of 'worker'. A further account of the nature of life transitions is provided by Adams *et al.* (1976), which describes the emotional adjustments that are required when individuals are faced with major personal change. Coping with and managing life change is also one of the key themes of social and life skills teaching.

Self-Awareness

Implementing career decisions is difficult without a clear idea of one's interests and abilities and values, and one of the main objectives of careers education is to foster clients' awareness of themselves in relation to jobs and work. It can take the form of a review of previous educational or work experiences and early influences on career thinking. It may be facititated by the use of occupational interest guides, values exercises or asking clients to write about their past achievements and future aspirations. Whatever method is used, the aim of this part is to help clients towards a clearer idea of themselves. As Law and Watts (1977) point out, the school curriculum itself has a part to play in identifying particular skills and abilities, such as language fluency, mathematical ability and creativity, particularly in subjects like English, art and music. It is less likely, however, that topics such as clarification of persona! values, or reviewing family influences on individuals' aspirations will appear in the traditional secondary school curriculum, and it may be the task of careers education programmes to introduce this kind of topic. From a practitioner's point of view, it is probably true to say that this particular objective is the one that is most difficult to achieve because of the difficulty of identifying suitable materials, of evaluating the learning outcomes effectively, and because of the element of risk it may pose for tutor/counsellor and client in exploring potentially sensitive areas such as self, relationships and personal identity.

Opportunity Awareness

By contrast, stimulating an increased awareness of different kinds of work, education and training opportunity is probably the easiest objective for careers specialists to achieve and has traditionally been the main concern of school-based careers education programmes. Talks by visiting employers, films on different occupational areas and information sheets on job families are all ways in which this kind of objective can be met. The principal difficulty for the careers specialist is one of selectivity — which of a vast range of materials and resources to use for particular client groups. The important dimension against which this kind of careers education activity can be set is one of the degree of involvement it demands of the students. The passive viewing of television programmes in class may well be more manageable but less rewarding than students' active involvement in case studies, group discussion or business games (see Figure 2.1)

Figure 2.1. Methods of Increasing Opportunity Awareness

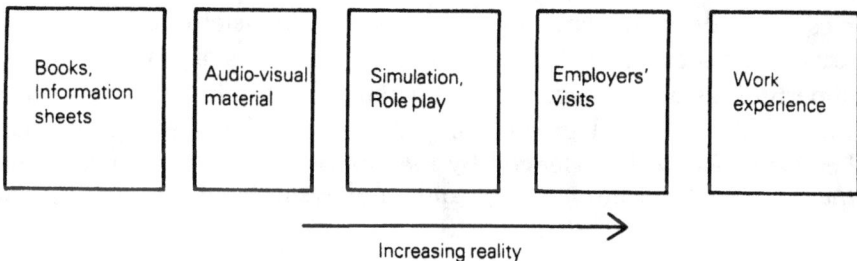

| Books, Information sheets | Audio-visual material | Simulation, Role play | Employers' visits | Work experience |

Increasing reality →

In simple terms, a visit to a hospital or bank may provide a more stimulating and powerful learning experience for students than a video on careers in banking. A further discussion on this topic is provided in Chapter 4 which looks in more detail at the role of career and occupational information.

Careers Education and the Secondary Curriculum

The major focus for careers education in this country has been the secondary school curriculum and in the main careers education has been concerned with the transition from school to work of the statutory age school leaver. Early approaches and provision for careers education in schools in England and Wales are documented in two publications, DES Survey 18, *Careers Education in Secondary Schools*, and the Schools Council Working Paper 40, *Careers Education in the 1970's*. Both reports described the range of school-based careers activities; the facilities that could be made available to careers teachers; and examples of good practice that were then available. Survey 18 concluded, however, that:

> The concept of careers education as that element in the school programme more especially concerned with preparation for living and working in the adult world is not at present generally accepted or put into practice except by a minority of schools.

Both publications described a situation in which careers education had been implemented in schools on a patchy and piecemeal basis, with some schools paying considerable attention to the topic, with others failing to give any prominence to the idea. There was, it seemed, no universal acceptance that careers education should be a permanent component in the school curriculum. Perhaps not surprisingly neither report attempted to pay attention to the exact nature of the careers education curriculum and its objectives, presumably because of the poorly developed state of the art at that time. What is clear, however, in retrospect, is that in their early forms, school-based careers programmes were designed largely for average ability, statutory age school leavers and focused on increasing pupils' awareness of job and training opportunities and the general preparation of pupils for the world of work. The place and growing importance of careers education, has, however, been acknowledged by the Government's *A Framework for the School Curriculum* (1980) and in the successor document, *The School Curriculum* (1981).

> ... The Secretaries of State consider that substantial attention should be given at the secondary stage to the relationship between school work and preparation for working life.... Particular attention should be given to the place of careers education and guidance for all pupils, including the most able

and those in the sixth form, planned in conjunction with the work of the careers service.

Systematic careers education should begin not later than the third secondary year and it is normally desirable that it should occupy a specific place in the timetable. Periods of work experience and work observation can be useful for pupils of all levels of ability. (*The Schools Curriculum*, 1981).

The HMI Survey, *Aspects of Secondary Education in England* (1979), gives some evidence of the extent to which careers education has developed in schools. Of nearly 400 schools surveyed, half offered a timetabled careers programme to all pupils in fourth and fifth years. Many more pupils received some careers education, either in year 4 or year 5, except in grammar schools, in which 70 per cent of all pupils received no formal careers education whatsoever (see Table 2.1)

Table 2.1. Provision of Careers Education Programmes

Year 4	
Extent of provision	*All schools*
All pupils	51%
Some	12%
None	37%

Year 5	
Extent of provision	*All schools*
All pupils	49%
Some	15%
None	36%

N = 384

Source: Aspects of Secondary Education in England (1979) HMI Report, London, HMSO. Reproduced with permission of the Controller, HMSO.

The survey also provides interesting data on the method of organization and timetabling of careers education in the curriculum and identifies four distinct methods of implementation, the most popular of which seems to be the allocation of one period a week for pupils in years 4 and 5 (see Table 2.2).

Where careers education was offered as a curriculum component, the four different types of interview were:

1 timetabled provision of one period a week or more;

Table 2.2. The Timetabling of Careers Education

Timetabled arrangements	Fourth year only	Fifth year only	Years 4 and 5
More than one period	5	4	13
One period per week	14	14	61
Rotational	9	3	32
Part of a broader course	0	1	29
Replacement Systems	2	1	12
Hybrid systems	0	0	17

Source: *Aspects of Secondary Education in England* (1979) HMI Report London, HMSO. Reproduced with permission of the Controller, HMSO.

2   rotational provision, in which careers education is blocked with other subjects;

3   a planned component of broader programmes, for example, general studies, designed for living;

4   a replacement or substitution system in which careers education is substituted on an occasional or more frequent basis with other subjects.

Given the pressure on curriculum time, particularly for examination classes, it is hardly surprising that careers teachers and coordinators have had to take flexible approaches in attempting to establish careers education as a regular curriculum component.

Problems of Implementation

The school-based careers education curriculum has conventionally centred on the decision points which affect the majority of pupils. For example, third year students faced with subject options, fifth year leavers groups faced with course choice and job seeking, have provided an immediate focus on the development of careers education inputs to the curriculum. Until recently, therefore, most school-based careers education has been telescoped into two years of secondary schooling, with comparatively little attention being paid to the needs of students on academic A-level courses in the sixth form. As a consequence, careers specialists have had to work in a comparatively short time scale with fourth and fifth year students to have any significant impact in helping students with the themes of choice and transition. This has made particular demands on the work of careers specialists and has, in part, led to the emphasis on team approaches to careers guidance activity, with a number of teaching staff with a secondary responsibility for careers, all giving support to the careers coordinator.

As the results of the HMI survey show, careers education is still far from being a universally accepted addition to the school curriculum and like other 'minority' subjects, such as health and social education, does not always command timetable time. For many careers teachers, the most frustrating aspect of their work is their inability to claim timetable time for their subject, in the face of competition from subject specialists who teach examination subjects. On this issue, as with many others to do with school resources, much depends on the active support and backing of the headteacher.

As a result of this difficulty in claiming sufficient time for careers education, careers teachers have been forced to adopt various approaches aimed at getting at least some of their message across to their students. At a very basic level, this can mean substituting careers for another timetabled subject. Often careers staff admit to using their first subject, for example, geography or religious studies to teach some careers, working on the principle, presumably, that some input is better than none at all. At a more established level, careers education can often form part of a programme of general or social education concerned with a wide variety of personal, political and moral issues. In schools in which there is a commitment to active tutorial work or a coordinated guidance approach, form tutor periods may be used to raise a range of issues to do with interpersonal relationships, study skills and decision-making.

Another approach which is widely canvassed and yet appears to make little headway is that of the integration of careers education across the entire curriculum. According to this model, it is possible to infuse many curriculum subjects with some or all of the careers education objectives, as described earlier. Using English lessons to teach the job application letters, maths to teach skills in personal budgeting and finance and geography to identify local industries and employment, should, in theory, provide an opportunity to infuse careers education objectives throughout the curriculum. In practice, the tasks of coordination and ensuring teacher participation seem to raise particular problems in ensuring the development of this form of infused approach.

Leavers' programmes in special schools provide a very interesting example of the way the entire curriculum of the last two years of special education is geared to the idea of starting work and earning a living. Despite the attraction of an infusion approach, it seems clear that careers education, as a single curriculum subject, is likely to remain the most common method of introducing 'careers' to the secondary school curriculum (see Figure 2.2).

If careers education is difficult to implement successfully from a curricular and organizational point of view, it also raises difficulties concerned with teaching method and delivery. As Law and Watts (1977) point out in their study of six secondary schools and their careers education programmes, considerable attention is often paid to one particular objective, that of increasing students' awareness of job and career opportunities. Schools less frequently manage to meet other possible objectives of the careers curriculum concerned with increasing students' self-awareness, or encouraging students to learn how to make decisions or cope with eventual transition from school to work. There seem to be two principal reasons for this, one concerned with the approaches adopted by individual teachers and another to do with the organizational context within which they work.

The teaching methods required to meet the curriculum objectives described above are essentially different in emphasis from those required in traditional teaching situations. They rely far more heavily on group discussion and participatory classroom activity. Many careers education materials are designed for task or syndicate groups, which work on their own, often independently of the teacher. Topics such as *identifying the factors involved in job choice* or *ways of coping with unemployment* may well be raised in small group discussion, with the main emphasis on students learning from each other's experience, rather than listening to an input of information by the teacher or tutor. It is also quite possible that at some point the lesson may become overtly less to do with 'careers' and more to do with the group of students and their aspirations both individually and as a group.

Some teachers, of course, will not feel comfortable with the facilitator role and will be far happier if cast in the role of instructor or subject expert. For some, encouraging open classroom discussion may be altogether too risky, particularly if the school itself does not encourage group discussion and active learning of this kind. It may be, for example, that the students themselves may be unused to working in a manner which enables them to disclose themselves and talk freely in classroom settings. In this case the organizational context and school ethos may well inhibit the development of careers education activity,

Figure 2.2   A School-Based Careers Education Curriculum

Year	Topic	Main objectives
Three	Interest and individual abilities	Self-awareness
	Choices and decisions	Decision learning
	Relationship between curriculum subjects and occupational areas	Preparation of students for subject options
Four	Personal values and occupational interests	Self-awareness — preparation for choice and adjustment
	The nature and organization of work and leisure	Opportunity awareness — a general perspective
	Occupational fields and employment levels	Decision learning
	Qualification routes and career entry points	
	Career decision-making	
Five	Job search and self-presentation skills	Opportunity and self-awareness
	Making applications and coping with interviews	To coach and give confidence to students facing selection procedures
	Identifying specific employment/ training opportunities	To help students prepare to find work
	Financial survival skills: money management	Transition learning — focusing on the process of starting work
	Adjustment to work: the working day; keeping a job; gaining promotion/change	
	Employment legislation	Encouraging students to anticipate future changes in their lives
	Employee rights and responsibilities	
	The function of unions	Equip students with information and ideas about basic survival skills
	Identifying alternatives to paid employment: voluntary work, state training schemes	
	Coping with unemployment, managing and using time effectively	

particularly if silence in class is the behavioural norm. It is often for these reasons that the self-awareness and decision learning parts of the careers education curriculum take second place to those concerned with job knowledge. In terms of classroom management it is easier to show a video on 'careers in engineering' than it is to use decision-making exercises on 'my choice of a job or course'. The second difficulty faced by careers teachers wanting to implement careers education is the structure of the school timetable. Many of the careers education methods described here rely heavily on role play, simulation and other non-traditional forms of classroom method which may require a double period to be carried out effectively. The amount of time available will, therefore, be a constraint on what can be achieved.

In this respect, teaching careers education shares many of the same methodological problems as the teaching of social and life skills. As Hopson and Scally (1981) point out, the skills and approaches required for groupwork are very different from those required for formal classroom teaching (see Figure 2.3). In group work method greater emphasis is placed on the role of the teacher as facilitator rather than instructor, imparting subject knowledge. More emphasis is likely to be given to peer learning resulting from participatory classroom method, in which students learn from and alongside their peers as well as the teacher/facilitator. The fundamental assumptions underlying the use of small group work are that by

— interacting with each other;
— taking part in well defined participatory exercises, for example, simulation and role play;
— using the group, teacher and community as resource,

students will become more aware of themselves, develop social skills, grow in self-confidence and be left with the belief that every group member can plan and be responsible for his or her own personal and career development.

These assumptions, of course, can pose a sizeable challenge to teachers who are used to, and happy with, formal didactic teaching, since the use of small group discussion method raises a host of issues to do with classroom management and control, the authority of the teacher and the risks involved in deviating from normal pedagogic practice. This in part explains why it is often safer, for example, for teachers to invite an outside speaker into school to talk about going for a job interview than it is to undertake a classroom simulation on the recruitment and selection process.

Figure 2.3.   A Comparison of Formal and Group Work Methods in the Classroom

Subject teaching by formal classroom methods	*Personal and interpersonal skill learning in small groups and in a classroom*
Emphasis more on presenting information than on experiencing events — often passive learners.	Emphasis on experiencing and learning from sharing one's own experience and hearing that of others — learners are active.
Information given is largely about the experience of others.	The focus is on the ideas and experience of the participants. The teacher is helping to structure the learning for them.
Emphasis is on the subject or topic being dealt with.	The subject *is* the participants — they are learning about themselves and each other in different contexts.
Success is often measured by the student's ability to represent information previously presented by the teacher or collected from books.	Individuals are encouraged to see success in terms of self-awareness and skill development, bringing increased self-assessment, self-confidence, and more effective performance in a variety of arenas of life.
The teacher is the 'expert' — learning flows from him. Teachers teach — students learn.	Each individual is unique and, as such, has something to offer others. Each person, including the teacher, has something to teach and something to learn.
The teacher's 'expertise' rests on academic record in a particular subject.	The teacher's whole personality, opinions, experiences, skills, values, weaknesses, etc., are used in presenting the whole person as a member of the group.
Questions are focused on testing listener's understanding of subject.	Questions are focused on assisting listeners to understand themselves and each other more.
Teacher is regarded as of secondary importance to subject being studied. Teacher sets work which students do.	Teacher uses self as a model — using appropriate self-disclosure and own experience as a model. Often does the same work as the students.
Feedback given only by teacher. Emphasis in feedback is on correctness of information.	Feedback from a variety of sources. Emphasis in feedback is on variety of reactions of other people.

Teacher as instructor — giving the lesson.	Teacher as facilitator — offering a format/structure to assist student learning.
Teacher decides content and method of learning.	Teacher attempts to build contract regarding what will be learnt and how it will be learnt. Ground rules are agreed and established for the way the groups will operate.
Confidentiality regarding what is said in classroom is not seen as a significant concern.	Confidentiality regarding classroom statements needs to be accepted by students and teacher.
Possibly little relevance for whole school or college system of what is taught or learnt.	Probably significant implications for the rest of the system of what is learnt and *how* it is learnt.
Little peer learning.	Possibly a great deal of peer learning.
Probably little need for parents and other staff to be informed.	Likely to be important that parents and other staff are kept informed of work planned.
Teacher is usually teaching the whole class as one group.	Teacher uses a variety of subgroups to increase participation.

Source: Copyright © 1981 McGraw-Hill Book Co. (UK) Ltd. From Hopson and Scally, *Lifeskills Teaching*. Reproduced by permission of the publisher.

In a very real sense the problem for those teaching careers education is that it is a part of the curriculum which is both student and subject centred. A central focus will therefore be on where individuals and groups of students are in their career development and career thinking. The timing of different activities in the academic year, the pacing of individual lessons will become key considerations and attention will need to be carefully focused on what seems relevant to the student group. Highly participative careers education sessions, for example, on career decision-making will depend for their success partly on the readiness and receptiveness of the particular group of students. At the same time, however, there are aspects of the careers education programme — the subject centred elements — which can be introduced to all pupils at almost any time. Topics such as the structure of local employment, the role of unions and management or the nature of unemployment, which are less student centred, can therefore be more flexibly timetabled.

In summarizing the development of careers education in schools several points can be made:

— Careers education is generally accorded an importance in direct relationship to the academic ability of the pupils. Lower ability groups generally have greater access to careers education than those in upper ability bands who are likely to take public examinations. In some 11–18 secondary schools, the careers coordinator's responsibility rests with fourth and fifth year students, while sixth form tutors and occasionally head-teachers take responsibility for.... A-level students and their applications etc. to higher education. Careers education is seldom undertaken with 'academic' sixth formers.

— It is implemented most commonly as a subject-based curriculum, with a specific body of knowledge, rather than infused into the existing subject range. It can however be timetabled and 'packaged' in a number of different ways, depending on the school.

— Even when student centred, careers education is likely to reflect the values of the school and schooling and to point, implicitly to the relationship between academic success and the ability to find satisfactory work.

— Careers education in schools has developed as a response to the need to prepare students for the world of work, and the school to work transition. In future, it seems likely that careers education will have a greater emphasis on preparation for the world of further education, training and non-work.

Careers Education in Further Education

It may seem surprising that careers education is developing in colleges of further education and technical colleges with their strong traditions of vocational education and technical training. Recently, however, with the expansion of general education in further education and the developments in the provision of the Youth Training Scheme for the 16–19 age group, many students entering the further education sector have no clear vocational commitment, or if they do have such a commitment are finding it increasingly difficult to secure full-time work at the end of their courses. Moreover, student numbers have increased steadily in the last ten years, particularly those on full-time courses of study. With this kind of development in the FE sector it is not surprising that continuing attention is being paid to the vocational counselling needs of students of this particular age group.

In the context of further education, this increased need has been met by the provision of college-based careers counsellors and in some areas by the appointment of full-time lecturers in Careers Education. A further focus for careers education-like activity has been provided by the development of social and life skills teaching, particularly with those on YOP courses. In future it seems likely that social and life skills training will become an integrated component of many of the training programmes under the Youth Training Scheme.

A definitive statement of the rationale for life skills teaching is provided by Hopson and Scally (1981). Under the heading of life skills they include a number of personal competencies, which the authors suggest can be fostered by appropriate curricula. These include:

> survival and personal development skills, for example, problem solving, decision-making;
> communication and relationship skills, for example, being assertive;
> study skills, for example, using time effectively and developing study habits;
> skills for work, for example, job search and job retention skills;
> domestic skills, for example, managing a home, parenting;
> leisure and community skills, for example, how to use leisure time.

It can be seen that the objectives that Hopson and Scally set for life skills teaching share some similarities with those set by Watts and Law for careers education, particularly those concerned with decision-making and skills for obtaining and keeping jobs. As a rough generalization, however, it may be seen that life skills teaching embodies a far wider range of concerns than the narrower vocational perspective provided by a careers education approach.

In a survey of existing social and life skills training, Stanton *et al.* (1980) have distinguished seven models of social and life skills teaching currently operative:

1 a Deficiency Model which assumes that certain basic deficiencies for example, in numeracy or interpersonal skills, can be remedied;

2 a Competency Model with an emphasis on task centred learning and mastery of specific skills, for example, explaining oneself clearly, communicating effectively;

3 an Information-Based Model which assumes that information giving is a necessary condition for social and life skills develop-

ment, for example, information about how to claim sickness benefit is a necessary step in actually obtaining it;

4   a Socialization Model to do with the development of 'appropriate' attitudes and values, for example, to encourage students to take a responsible attitude to work and leisure;

5   an Experimental Model in which open ended experiences and activities are considered useful in developing capacities, the nature of which are not clearly specified, for example, outward bound courses, community action;

6   a Reflective Model concerned with helping students reflect on their experiences and perceive relationships between events, for example, encouraging students to review their cognitive processes, to make sense of facts or interpret data in new ways;

7   a Counselling Model, which concentrates on Bloom's 'Affective Domain', to do with the sharing of individual and group experiences to achieve greater self-awareness and insight.

As McGuire and Priestley (1981) point out, social skills training owes much of its development to social learning theory and behaviourist theories of learning; in practice, social skills programmes have emphasized that appropriate behaviours can be learned by modelling and rehearsal. It follows that much of the emphasis in life skills training is on personal problem solving, on coping with problems of interpersonal relationships, managing money or finding and keeping work. Arguably, however, there are some features common to both careers education and social and life skills programmes both in curriculum content and in method. In the context of further education, however, much of the careers education presently undertaken reflects exactly the same range of objectives as careers in secondary schools. The themes of job search, career decision-making, workers' rights and responsibilities are as much a part of the further education careers curriculum as they are of the schools curriculum described earlier. The main difference is that in further education there would seem to be fewer timetable constraints and the opportunity for careers workers to carry out work with a range of different courses and client groups — O- and A-level groups, vocational preparation courses, full-time vocational diploma courses and so on.

Careers Education in Higher Education

It may be a commonly held assumption that students in higher education must, by definition, be more fluent and competent than most at handling life and career decisions. What evidence there is, however, suggests that this is clearly not the case. Indeed, Watts (1977) has argued that the higher education experience is *dysfunctional* for most students in the extent to which it prepares them for a work role. Many higher education institutions, he argues, embody a value system which differs from most work environments and their departments and courses refuse to accept that vocational exploration is part of their function. Finally, because students are, in the main, removed from their home community, they can be alienated from the adult role-models against which they can evaluate themselves. The higher education process itself, then, can hinder the development of a student's occupational self-concept.

Recent evidence from studies of graduate job mobility lends further support to the motion that many graduates lack a clear occupational identity. Parsons and Hutt (1981) found that 55 per cent of graduates change jobs within five years and half of these changes represent a complete change of occupation. They conclude that for some graduates the change represents a transfer to a different sector of the economy, but ' . . . for others a realistic assessment of their abilities and aspirations may only be possible after two or more years work experience.'

In the light of the above and similar previous findings it is interesting to review the past assumptions of the various careers guidance and counselling services available to students in higher education. Traditionally careers guidance services in higher education have largely assumed that their graduates needed little help with career decision-making and have provided, in many cases, fairly sophisticated placement and appointments services. Indeed, much of the activity of careers services is still devoted to job information and placement and seeks to promote 'opportunity awareness' (Law and Watts, 1977) to the virtual exclusion of any other careers education objectives.

Increasingly, however, faced with rapidly changing employment conditions, increasing numbers of clients and the impact of alarming levels of unemployment, careers advisers and counsellors have begun to seek other ways of meeting the needs of their clients. A need to feel more cost and time effective in their work, or a genuine wish to work with groups of students as well as individuals, have led many practitioners towards a major re-evaluation of their assumptions about their guidance and placement roles. They are increasingly seeking an educational rationale for their work and are attempting to meet the other tasks of careers education by encouraging students to consider the move from higher education to work as a learning process in itself, in which attention has to be paid to self-awareness, decision learning and transition learning.

The growth of interest in careers education is well documented in the AGCAS Register of Careers Education Activities (Priddle, 1979); since that publication increasing numbers of practitioners have started to take initiatives in this field. An analysis of the entries in ROCEA, however, begs the question whether there can be further development of the careers education initatives already taken. Noticeably, most of the work presently undertaken reflects a single base line curriculum objective — that of enhancing skills in employment seeking and employability by the introduction, for example, of selection workshops. While there have been attempts to promote a broader set of objectives, in terms of career planning and personal re-evaluation, much of the work to date is concerned with preparing students for a yet more competitive employment market. Furthermore, an analysis of the programming of the careers education activities undertaken so far shows that they are carried out with little support from tutorial and lecturing staff, are external to students' courses of study (using free timetable time or staged at weekends) and have, therefore, little impact on the higher education curriculum. Many practitioners have, as a consequence, begun to question whether there will be a stage of development at which, instead of providing a dietary supplement of vocational exploration for needy students, the higher education curriculum itself can begin to be infused with elements that one might describe as 'careers education'.

Any sustained attempt at implementing careers education of necessity brings the careers adviser/counsellor into direct contact with teaching and faculty staff, at a time when the political challenges to the higher education system are making staff sensitive about work roles and their boundaries. However, our experience at Brighton, with three different courses suggests that it is possible to link a careers education programme with an existing academic course of study and that a fusion of interests is possible between the teaching and careers counselling staff. The concern of course leaders with the viability of course programmes and course evaluation can be matched with the careers counsellor's concern for individual students and their confidence in making a satisfactory transition to employment or further study, to produce a course-based careers education programme. The model presented in Figure 2.4 illustrates the way in which stand-alone careers education inputs became integrated course components with corresponding changes in attendance style accreditation and ownership. Many

Figure 2.4.   Careers Education Progammes: A Curriculum Infusion Approach

	Ad hoc initiative ⟶	Integrated programme
Format	Single/multiple ⟶ sessions	Series of timetabled sessions
Attendance style	Voluntary ⟶	Compulsory course component
Location	Based outside ⟶ courses	Course-based
Ownership	Careers adviser ⟶ counsellor	Course tutor in collaboration with careers adviser
Accreditation	⟶	Accreditation by course validating, for example, CNAA, BEC

of the changes listed have resulted in ultimate gains for the careers counsellor, particularly in terms of forging permanent links with teaching departments and, as Watts (1977) has suggested, have created a more central role for careers counselling work in the institution. On reflection, there may have been some losses in terms of the style of the careers education programme, perhaps with changing from a personal and experiential approach to one that has a more didactic tone, but this is compensated by the increased opportunity for individual counselling that careers education programmes generate.

Curriculum Objectives

The specific curriculum objectives obviously vary from programme to programme. What is clear, however, is that the major benefit of an integrated careers education programme is the chance to broaden the range of curriculum objectives — to go beyond job seeking and employability, by linking into the objectives of the student's main programme of study. With each course of study, a broadly-based and integrated programme can be negotiated between careers counsellor and degree course leader, and consequently the careers education programme can be styled to match the underlying rationale of the degree course.

In the case of the Enabling Studies Programme (see Figure 2.5) the specific careers education objectives of helping students establish themselves as artists/craftsmen are entirely compatible with the overall course aim. It should be stressed, however, that designing bespoke career development programmes for individual degree or diploma courses is not a once and for all activity, but involves a constant process of review and adaption to meet the needs of different student groups.

Figure 2.5.   An Example of an Integrated Careers Education Programme

Degree course	BA Three Dimensional Design
Principal aim	To produce artists/craftsmen
Careers education programme objectives:	— to encourage students to review their personal skills and work values — to examine the process of setting up as an artist/craftsman, for example: — costing and marketing work — finding workshop space, legal and financial implications of self-employment — to explore range of occupational opportunities — invite students to set short- and long-term work objectives
Title of course component	'Enabling Studies Programme'
Programming and method	Two-term seminar programme; final year: small-group discussion and workshops

Careers Education As a Total, Unifying Approach to Careers Work

In many ways a careers education approach represents a new departure in careers work in that it sees the encouragement of personal learning as the main objective of the careers practitioner. Vocational guidance and traditional advisory models of careers work have, in general, centred on the giving of expert advice about the 'best' course of action for the client to take. In a careers education approach to careers work the main emphasis is on helping clients to learn how to make career decisions, establish good work relationships, and be successful at job interviews. In attempting to find a unifying definition for careers education and to understand the assumptions underlying its recent development, it is helpful to review the theoretical assumptions to careers work described earlier. For, just as the vocational guidance interview and the counselling interview owe much to the theoretical assumptions upon which they are based, so careers education has its origins in psychological explanations and developmental theories of careers choice. If we accept that in choosing a career or starting work we are making a statement about the kind of person we are or would like to be — what Super (1957) calls implementing a self-concept — and, furthermore, that this is a process which will continue throughout life and is intimately related to our personal development, then we may also accept that it is possible to support and encourage this development in our clients. We might go further and argue that it is possible to help clients learn to identify and adjust to the different stages of this developmental process. It is precisely this kind of learning that careers education seeks to facilitate.

Whereas 'trait and factor' and talent matching approaches to occupational choice and placement (see Figure 2.6), which seek to secure an adequate fit between individual traits and job factors, are implemented in practice by diagnostic, vocational guidance interviews, self-concept and developmental theories suggest an approach to careers work which helps clients achieve certain steps towards further learning and vocational maturity. In this sense, careers education is an overall approach to careers work which seeks to help clients learn to implement career plans and decisions, not just at one particular stage but throughout their lives. Careers education can therefore be seen to share an important set of assumptions common to the counselling interview —

Figure 2.6.   The Implications for Careers Practitioners of Different Theoretical Approaches to Career Development

Theoretical approach to career development	Task for the practitioner	Methodology
Talent matching	Diagnostic guidance	Guidance interviews
Developmental, self-concept and decision-making theories	Educational	Careers education and counselling

that of the fostering of personal autonomy and enabling clients to act for themselves on the basis of their own awarenesses and decisions. Careers programmes and school guidance activities can be based on careers education objectives. Careers conventions, job talks, work experience programmes, employer visits can all be assessed in terms of the personal learning that they provide for the students taking part. A work experience placement, or indeed, holiday or Saturday job, may provide students with:

> insights and awarenesses of job opportunities;
> experience of working conditions and environments;
> sampling of various work tasks;
> exposure to different work values and occupational identities;

and therefore may accomplish some or all four of the objectives of self and opportunity awareness and decision and transition learning. Equally, a career planning workshop for adults faced with mid-career change which includes topics such as,

> a review of past work and educational experiences and achievements;
> a statement of present relationships and circumstances;
> an analysis of personal abilities, needs and values; and
> an evaluation of further career prospects

is in much the same way as a work experience placement providing an opportunity for individuals to learn about themselves in relation to work, although in this example there is a particular emphasis on reviewing and evaluating past experience and setting goals for the future.

A careers education approach, then, represents a move away from traditional advice and information giving models of careers guidance. It affirms that career choice and decision-making are not necessarily concerned with one single life event but with a continual process of personal change and learning which takes place over a life span. Accordingly, individuals are likely to be constantly reassessing their choices and decisions as their careers develop. What seems like an interesting, exacting job one day, may, two years later, appear routine and predictable, suggesting the need to reappraise one's position. The personal skills that are required for planning and implementing job change at the age of 35 are essentially the same kind of skills that 16-year-old school leavers require when attempting to find work for the first time. For in both cases there is a need to:

prepare for change and anticipate the future (transition learning);
review one's personal abilities, interests and values (self-awareness);
find out more information about alternative courses of action (occupational/opportunity awareness);
prepare to make a career decision or choice from the alternatives available (decision learning).

I have argued the case for careers education as a unifying approach to all aspects of careers work, but the term 'careers education' continues to pose problems for those who seek to define it. The word 'career' in contemporary English usage carries with it the notion of a steady and stable progression in a single occupation. In essence, it seems to describe what happens to the middle-class professional, rather than describing the lot of the majority of the population who simply have jobs, or even no job at all. It therefore seems acceptable to describe the work of a doctor or professional engineer as a career, but what of the shop assistant's work or that of the telephonist? At the same time 'career' is still used largely to describe paid employment, rather than embrace all kinds of work, paid and unpaid work in the home, etc. If the concept of careers education is to have currency in future, it seems likely that it will be concerned with preparation not just for work, but also for training and further study, the use of leisure and non-work. It may still be concerned with preparation for working life, but work in its very broadest sense, not simply that which equates with paid employment and jobs.

Chapter 3

The Helping Interview

There are many ways of helping people with their career decisions and choices. School- or college-based careers education programmes, career development courses for adults in mid-career, the use of self-help materials on career planning are all examples of the ways in which careers practitioners can help their clients clarify their career decisions. However, the main vehicle for careers work in any educational setting remains the one-to-one interview between careers practitioner and client. The aim of this chapter is to describe two contrasting approaches to interviewing: the vocational guidance and the helping or counselling interview, and to review the theoretical assumptions which underlie them — assumptions which, for the most part, affect the differing theoretical perspectives on the nature of career development. Whereas, for example, the vocational guidance interview derives in the main from talent matching theories of occupational choice and placement, counselling approaches derive far more from developmental perspectives and the notion that individuals do not make one single career decision at a particular time, but act out a series of choices and decisions over a life span.

The chapter also attempts to document the way in which the notion of the vocational guidance interview has given way to that of the helping or counselling interview (Crites, 1974) which forms part of the careers counselling process. It also provides an indication, in practical terms, of what makes the helping interview effective.

The Vocational Guidance Interview

One of the implications in practical terms of the talent matching approaches outlined in Chapter 1 is that as a result of a careers interview, the interviewer should be able to make some kind of assessment and recommendation of the kind of work or training the client should enter. A match should be made between the abilities, interests and aptitudes of the client with the demands of a particular occupation. Indeed, this is often a major expectation of clients seeking vocational guidance — that they will be given a clear idea of the career or occupational area they might expect to enter. According to this model of the careers interview, the interviewer, equipped with accurate biographical data, aptitude test or interest guide results, is expected, after an extended interview session, to make the most accurate assessment possible of the level and field of occupation at which the client is likely to be successful. In many ways it shares many of the characteristics of the selection interview carried out by personnel staff and recruitment agencies.

The approach, of course, raises a particular set of expectations of the interviewer in the careers interview — that the interviewer should have a wealth of knowledge of existing employment opportunities, be skilled in diagnosis and assessing the potential of the interviewee. It assumes also that much of the interview will be concerned with fact finding by the interviewer and that after the fact finding stage the interviewer will be able to provide information and advise about the most appropriate course of action for the interviewee.

Implicit in the vocational guidance approach to interviews is the need for objectivity in assessment. Interviewers, it is argued, are fallible and in order to reduce the margin error in the interview assessment, it becomes necessary to employ psychometric measures — tests of interest, personality and aptitude — to provide empirically derived data on which to base the interviewers assessment. The test data are then used to advise and even persuade the client of the best course of action. The use of psychological tests of this kind is evidence of the influence of both differential and occupational psychology in the origins of the vocational guidance interview, and it is interesting to note in passing that many of the vocational guidance agencies in this country which exist outside the educational system often employ staff with psychological training as consultants and advisers.

As Daws (1968) suggests, however, the vocational guidance interview provides a very particular set of role expectations. The careers specialist, as the acknowledged expert, is expected to provide the correct diagnosis, rather like a general practitioner in medical practice. The interviewee, on the other hand, is likely to be the passive recipient of the prescribed course of action.

> ... Once it is accepted that vocational guidance is basically a matching process, certain other features of the process follow

more or less inevitably. It follows that there will be a specialist to give information and advice and make recommendations. The most appropriate time to provide the service will obviously be just before the client must commit himself to an occupational choice, for then the necessary picture of the client's assets and requirements will be fully available and up to date. It also follows that for two reasons there will be only one 'specialist' handling the case and secondly an adviser needs to have the total picture of his client as well as complete knowledge of occupational requirements as a basis for his advisory and recommendatory decisions.

The need for the service obviously ceases when the client implements a recommended choice and that need will recur only if the client 'fails' in his job and needs to be advised about an alternative.

The distinguishing features of the vocational guidance interview (as shown in Figure 3.1) contrast with those of the helping or counselling interview. The main aim of the inteview is assessment of the inter-viewee and the outcome, as Daws suggests, is a recommendation which

Figure 3.1. Comparison between Vocational Guidance and Counselling Interviews

	Diagnostic guidance	Counselling interviews
Main aim	Assessment	Enabling the client
Nature of the interview	A one-off and once and for all interview	One of a series of helping encounters
Aids used	Extensive use of pre-interview forms and test results	Little use of screening or test material
Primary focus	Attention paid to biographical facts, for example, educational attainment and progress	Attention paid to client's feelings and percep-tions and internal frame of reference
Interview boundaries	Tightly maintained parameters to the interview	Likelihood that presenting problem will lead to discussion of other personal issues
Expected outcome	A recommendation to follow	Increased learning and awareness

the client is encouraged to follow. During the interview, the interviewer is likely to depend on the use of pre-interview forms and questionnaires supplied by the client, and by questioning and eliciting information, often by direct questioning, the interviewer will try to build up a picture of the interviewee before making a job recommendation. The helping or counselling interview, on the other hand, is based on an entirely different set of assumptions — the primary one being that the client has the power and ability to decide for himself about his career direction and that the interviewer's role is to facilitate and encourage the client's active use of careers information to make a decision, wisely, for himself. The interviewer behaviour which characterizes the helping interview is described in more detail later.

It is important at this stage to draw attention to the main implication of the vocational guidance interview for the client. The vocational guidance interview can be seen to rest on a largely static model of the way people manage and relate to their careers. It assumes that it is practically possible for an interviewer to get to know all about a given individual during the course of one or two interviews and perhaps encourages in the interviewee the belief, some would argue the largely erroneous one, that there is but one right job, one right course of action as long as the vocational guidance specialist can unearth it. It may also be seen to pay insufficient attention to the idea of change and development within the individual and therefore to fail to take into account the dynamic relationship between individuals and the work they do. Finally, it tends to place the interviewee in a passive and accepting mode, which may encourage him not to accept responsibility for his own career decisions and may not encourage clients to have confidence in making their own autonomous choices.

As Rogers (1942) observes in an early book, the diagnostic guidance interview not only takes away the client's responsibility for his or her own decisions, but is potentially disruptive of the client-counsellor relationship.

> When the counsellor assumes the information getting attitude which is necessary for the assembling of a good case history, the client cannot help feeling that the responsibility for the solution of his problems is being taken over by the counsellor.

One of the early frameworks for the diagnostic interview was provided by Rodger (1952). The Seven Point Plan was an attempt to provide a 'scientifically-defensible' framework for assessment during both employer selection and vocational guidance interviews. The seven points: physical make up, attainments, general intelligence, special aptitudes, interests, disposition and circumstances were intended as independent pointers for interviewers to ensure that their interviews were more than a superficial question and answer session. The aim was to give structure and depth to an interview, of which the principal task was clearly the assessment and appraisal of clients. With its emphasis on appraising client attributes, abilities and intelligence, it clearly demonstrates its origins in the 'trait and factor' or talent matching theories discussed in an earlier chapter.

That the Seven Point Plan should have such a major influence on careers work, and the professional practice of careers officers in particular, now seems surprising. It was used widely as the basis, and still is, for selection interviewing and, amongst some careers practitioners, for careers interviews. Rodger himself was aware that its use posed more problems for 'vocational advisers' than it did for those involved in selection. In a statement which clearly reflects the talent matching assumptions upon which it was based, Rodger admits:

> Associated with it [the plan] is the much greater difficulty the vocational adviser experiences in making allowances for his inability to judge how well a person will 'fit in' with people with whom he will in fact have to work.

Rodger was all too aware of the task facing careers practitioners, and the almost impossible task both conceptually and practically of fitting the right person to the right job as the result of a vocational guidance interview. There are many, of course, encouraged largely by the claims of occupational psychology, who still advance the idea that it is in the professional interviewer's power to match people to jobs successfully in this way. Kline (1975) asserts that vocational guidance must consist of fitting men to jobs' and acknowledges that interviews have a role in tempering the results of psychometric tests! Clarke (1980) laments the lack of research evidence to support the vocational guidance interview.

Many of the early evaluatory studies of the work of the careers service were based on the assumption that careers officers were working according to a talent matching rather than a developmental model, and therefore attempted to show the relationship between the careers officer's recommendations at interview and the kind of work entered by the client. Not surprisingly, the relationship between recommendations and jobs entered was found to be weak, although some positive relationship was found for a relationship between careers officer interviews and the length of stay in the first job — perhaps indicating that the careers interview had been helpful from the point of view of the client's transition from school to work (Cherry, 1974).

Early research also showed that whatever the purpose of the interview from the careers practitioner's point of view, the purpose from the client's point of view was seldom properly articulated. Research by Jahoda and Chalmers (1963), for example, showed that the students experienced the interview not as an interview, but as the seeking of information by the careers counsellor for what purpose they were often unsure. Clearly misconceptions about the use of the guidance interview were commonplace and, as Lloyd and Wilson (1980) point out, this still persists. The legacy of the diagnostic or vocational guidance model of interviewing still remains.

More recently a study by Bedford (1982b) uses a vocational guidance framework to analyze the process and outcomes of 680 careers officer interviews in 200 schools throughout the country. By using a standard framework based on the mnemonic FIRST:

Focus — how far has the student narrowed down options;
Information — how well informed is the student about career options;
Realism — how realistic is the student;
Scope — how aware is the student about the range of options available;
Tactics — to what extent has the student worked out the practical steps necessary to achieve his/her career objectives,

the investigation attempted to relate interviewer characteristics with the outcomes of the interview for the young person. The study relied on a diagnostic framework, but one which looked at the stage a client had reached in career thinking and to this extent considered the interviews from a developmental perspective. The results of the study have some interesting implications for careers practitioners and tutors of training courses. Some of the more salient points to emerge were as follows.

Four broad types of interview skills emerged which concerned:

1 summarizing and clarifying;
2 identify and meeting students' immediate needs;
3 establishing the purpose of the interview; and
4 creating a friendly and encouraging atmosphere.

From the observer's point of view, the factor most closely associated with an effective interview was that of creating a friendly encouraging atmosphere.

No statistically significant relationship was found between an interviewer's qualities and written sources of information, school reports, pre-interview questionnaires or previous interview notes.

Interviewers were more effective in helping students who were already more vocationally aware at the start of their interview (this finding points particularly to the importance of careers education).

The older the student, the more effective the interview; sixth former interviews were more effective than those with fifth years, which, in turn, were more effective than those with fourth year interviews.

Complete change in a student's orientation is unlikely to occur. Results generally indicated a narrowing down of options.

The interview was not seen as the most appropriate place to try to meet students' information needs.

The effectiveness of the interviews was directly dependent on the extent of contact between careers officer and school. Clinic interviews were more effective than 'cold canvassing' blanket interviews.

The results reflect many of the new practices in school-based careers work and to this extent may not prove surprising to many school-based careers practitioners. What is clear, however, is that the results lend a good deal of support to the conceptualization of a careers interview as a helping or counselling interview rather than one which is based on a diagnostic guidance model. Establishing a friendly encouraging atmosphere, for example, is simply another way of describing the process of establishing rapport and accepting the client which is common to the helping interview and the careers counselling process. Allowing students to refer themselves for interview, characteristic of the 'clinic' approach described above, is again one of the preconditions for an effective helping interview. It is argued in the remainder of this chapter that the careers counselling interview is a more appropriate description for the more effective careers interviewing currently being practised in educational settings.

The Helping Interview

As work colleagues, friends or close relations, many of us will be asked at some time or other to share someone else's concerns and listen to his or her problems. On these occasions all that may be required is for us to listen or give an attentive ear rather than give advice or act on someone else's behalf. Listening and sharing may be sufficient to help the other person resolve his or her difficulties. As part of their work, teachers with pastoral responsibilities, youth workers and training supervisers may be faced with this situation frequently. Professional helpers in the fields of social work, counselling and careers counselling will spend much of their working lives in helping encounters of the kind described above; their training is concerned with developing their sensitivity and skills to ensure that their helping interviews are as effective and rewarding as possible for both themselves and their clients. As Brammer (1979) points out, however, there is no reason why some of these skills at least should not be developed by all people to some degree. Being able to listen attentively and hear other peoples' concerns is a normal part of an individual's interpersonal skills. The aim of the following pages is to show how the helping interview, in the context of careers counselling, can be made as effective as possible, and to point to the kinds of skills and behaviours that make for a successful interview.

A useful starting point is to consider how the interview originated. The chance encounter and conversation in the corridor or careers information room which develops into a lengthy helping interview may well have a very difficult quality to one which has arisen because a client or student has arranged to see a careers practitioner, having been referred by someone else. It is important, therefore, to be aware of the degree of voluntarism and genuine self-referral that exists prior to the helping interview. As we saw earlier, interviews are more likely to be effective when students and clients refer themselves. Secondly it is important to pay attention to the environmental circumstances. Most careers practitioners will have access to an interview room and the arrangement of furniture within it will have a bearing on the degree of visual contact there is between interviewer and interviewee. For example, an executive desk lodged between counsellor and client is unlikely to encourage the sense of understanding and rapport that is required. Comfortable chairs, on the other hand, with counsellor and client seated at the same eye level should ensure the optimal conditions for the interview. Significant background noise and continued interruptions will not facilitate the development and progress of the interview. For those new to relatively structured interviewing, attention usually focuses on what to say and what questions to ask. A number of texts deal with this topic in detail, but in brief it is probably worth emphasizing the need for the selective use of single, open ended questions for clarification and any fact finding, for example, 'How did you come to choose your A-level subjects?', which is far more likely to elicit a full response than, 'You were good at geography, weren't you?' The degree of open-endedness in the interview and the extent to which the interviewee feels able to talk will depend not only on the use of questions, but also on the degree to which he or she is able to relate to the interviewer and on the relationship that already exists between interviewer and client. Where there has been no previous contact, the interviewer may have to work hard to establish the degree of trust and confidence required on the part of the client.

One way of identifying the factors which make for an effective interview is to review an interview which in retrospect has been helpful to you. Begin by asking the question: 'What made it helpful?' Then move on to think of the behaviour of the interviewer, the kinds of interventions he or she made, your own feelings before and after the interview, and reflect on the nature of the interview outcome. Reflecting on your own experience in this way may provide a useful guide to the kinds of factors that contribute to a genuinely helpful interview. In addition, the checklist provided in Figure 3.2 is intended as a rough and ready guide to the process of the helping interview, focusing as it does on the behaviours, leads and responses of both interviewer and interviewee. To this extent, it focuses on the *process* of the interview and how it developed from beginning to end. It will also be important to review the *content* of the interview. In many helping interviews concerned with career choice and decision-making the content of the interview will show a temporal development which consists of a review of the client's past, in terms of his or her interests, values and experiences, a clarification of his or her present position in terms of immediate circumstances and situation and a plan for the client's future: a goal to reach, a plan to be implemented, a suggestion for future action. The content of the interview may well focus, therefore, on the interviewee's past, present and future.

With this in mind, a useful mnemonic for the helping interview, particularly when concerned with career planning and decision-making and choice, is:

Create an atmosphere which is congenial to the client and inter-
    viewer;
Identify needs and problems with the client;
Assess, with the client, the parameters of the situation;
Offer a framework in which clients can act for themselves.

By working through this sequence of steps, with interviewer and interviewee working together through each stage, it should be possible to provide the interviewee with a useful framework in which to operate. The initial phase will be dependent on the interview environment, the

Figure 3.2. *Checklist for the Helping Interview*

The process of the interview	Who initiated the helping interview?
	How did the discussion begin?
	What contract was defined by yourself and the client?
	How did the interview develop?
	How did it close?
The environmental circumstances	What atmosphere surrounded the interview?
	Did the room and seating provide optimal conditions for interviewing?
	Were there interruptions?
	Was there enough time?
Interviewer characteristics	How far were you able to create an atmosphere of trust and confidence?
	Did you accept and show liking for the client?
	How far did you understand the client and share his or her frame of reference?
	How far did you achieve any kind of empathy?
Interviewer characteristics	How ready was the client for the discussion?
	How much trust and confidence did the client show in you?
	How easy was it for the client to talk?
	How honest was the client in the relationship?
Interviewer behaviour	How relaxed and confident were you with your role in the encounter?
	Were you able to listen actively and respond fully to the client?
	What kind of questionning did you employ (open/closed; direct/indirect; single/multiple)?
	What other kind of behaviour responses did you make?
Interviewee behaviour	How did the client appear in the interview?
	What was the nature of the silences in the interview?
	Could the client talk about his/her feelings?
Interview outcomes	How was the interview left?
	Was there a need for referral or further meetings?
	What learning took place on your part, on the client's part?
	What gains were there from the helping encounter?

attitude and behaviour of the interviewer and the degree to which he or she is ready to make time for and welcome the client and establish a feeling of trust and confidence at an early stage in the interview.

The second stage consists of identifying and negotiating with the interviewee the reason why he/she has come for interview and to agree on the subject for discussion. This could at first appear no more than a simple request for information — 'I'd like to know how to get into banking' — or acknowledging a decision problem — 'I don't know whether to stay on at school or try and get a job' — or admitting to some confusion — 'I just don't know what to do when I leave'. Often the simple request for information may be a cover for considerable uncertainty on the client's part and it will be for the interviewer to establish the exact definition of the problem presented.

The third stage is again one of exploration and is concerned with helping the client assess all the relevant factors which have a bearing on the problem. In the case of a mature student entering higher education, for example, his or her circumstances and relationships with spouse and children may be seen as an influential factor in determining the place of study and hence choice of course. If the student is considering a vocational course, discussion may well also centre on the place work is likely to play in his or her life and competencies, values and interests and the appropriateness and relevance of any previous work experience. At the end of this assessment stage, it may be appropriate for the interviewer to order and synthesize all or some of the information presented by the client to increase further the interviewer's and client's understanding of the situation. This may be done by reflective statements such as, 'It sounds as though you really enjoyed your last two jobs because they involved a good deal of independence', or more confrontingly, 'I get the impression that in your job you've often found it difficult to cope with some of the demands made on you'. It is important that the summary should be mutually agreed between interviewer and client.

The final stage of the helping interview is often concerned with broadening the interviewee's view of the problem and providing suggestions for action. Suggesting ideas, providing information, setting goals and strategies for achieving them are characteristic of the final stage of the interview. This will not involve the interviewer in making a decision *for* the client, but helping the interviewee see how a decision can be arrived at and see the implications of various courses of action. In a helping interview concerned with career choice, this is the stage when often the interviewer's knowledge of the broad opportunity structure, entry requirements for different occupational areas and training routes will come into play, in providing suggestions for the interviewee to explore further. Referring clients to other sources of information, contacts and helping agencies may also be an appropriate outcome.

Skills for the Helping Interview

It will be clear to those who have had interviewing experience that there exists a hierarchy of interview skills, which reflects the ease with which they can be mastered. Skills concerned with listening and questioning, for example, may be comparatively easy to master. Those concerned with interpreting accurately what the client is saying or those concerned with problem solving may require considerable rehearsal and practice before they can be used successfully.

Those new to the idea of the helping interview may find it surprising that listening, particularly active listening, is the most fundamental of all interview skills. This implies paying attention to the content of what is being said and also to the way it is said, or 'listening with the third ear'. It means taking note of the interviewee's body language and posture; noting whether he or she is tense or relaxed, for example, and taking account of gestures and movement. The interviewee's tone of voice and other verbal behaviours, such as stammering or stuttering, will also provide important clues to the way the interviewee is feeling and his/her sense of ease in the interview situation. The body language of the interviewer, too, may help or hinder the development of the interview as much as any direct or indirect question. An interviewer who feels comfortable and relaxed may evoke a similar relaxed style on the part of the client.

In the helping interview the primary objective is to encourage the interviewee to talk, and active listening will provide encouragement for the client to continue with what he or she is saying and will help him or her to disclose thoughts and feelings.

As well as attending and listening in this way the interviewer will also want to clarify occasionally what is being said, perhaps by openly admitting cofusion — 'I'm not sure I understand what you said' — and by occasionally restating or paraphrasing what the interviewee has said to convey understanding. Some mention has already been made of the use of questions; interviews often begin with an open question such as, 'How can I help you?', or less directly, 'Can you say what you've come to see me about?' There are also other ways of leading the interview on to the next stage. Prompts, such as, 'it might be helpful if you said some more about your previous work experience', will encourage the client to focus on a particular topic and at the same time move the interview forward.

Another skill which is important for exploring the client's situation or problem is reflecting the content of what the interviewee is saying or his or her feelings — 'You've always wanted to study social sciences, but your parents were against the idea', may reflect what the interviewee has said and at the same time convince the interviewee that the interviewer or counsellor really does appreciate the situation. On occasions it will be necessary for the interviewer to cope with what may at first seem like embarrassing silences. There will be times, particularly in school-based careers interviews, when the interviewee will not want to talk or will only take part in the interview half-heartedly. Often this may be because the interviewee has been referred to the interviewer and it will be the task of the interviewer to explore the circumstances behind the referral and possibly suggest that the client come at some future time when ready. Certainly, the temptation to bombard the interviewee with questions or fill the vacuum with interviewer talk should be resisted. On many occasions simply being with the client in silence is an effective helping response, particularly midway through a helping interview when the client is constructively thinking through a particular statement he or she has made or possibly a reflection on the part of the interviewer, and when it is obvious that interviewer and interviewee are in contact with each other.

A useful analysis of helping interview skills is provided by Brammer (1979) who suggests that different skills are likely to be required, depending on the kind of helping interview. As Figure 3.3 shows, to help clients in a crisis, who, for example, may have suddenly been made redundant or faced with unexpected examination failure, the main need may be for counsellor skills of comforting and supporting. To help clients improve their study skills, on the other hand, or write convincing letters of application, or face a career decision, may, Brammer suggests, call for problem solving and behaviour changing skills on the part of the counsellor.

An interview framework of a different kind is provided by Egan (1975). This analyzes all helping encounters in terms of a three-phase model, which begins with *Exploration*, which relies primarily on the skills of attending, listening and focusing. During the second phase, *Understanding*, the counsellor will be concerned with summarizing what the interviewee had said and to reflect back thoughts and feelings which may help the interviewee see his or her problem from a different point of view. Other skills such as self-disclosure, confrontation and immediacy may be employed at this stage. Finally the third phase of

Figure 3.3.   Helping Skills

For understanding	For comfort and crisis utilization	For positive action

1 *Listening*
  1.1 Attending
  1.2 Paraphrasing
  1.3 Clarifying
  1.4 Perception
     checking
2 *Leading*
  2.1 Indirect leading
  2.2 Direct leading
  2.3 Focusing
  2.4 Questioning
3 *Reflecting*
  3.1 Feeling
  3.2 Content
  3.3 Experience
4 *Summarizing*
  4.1 Feeling
  4.2 Content
  4.3 Process
5 *Confronting*
  5.1 Describing feelings
  5.2 Expressing
     feelings
  5.3 Feeding back
  5.4 Meditating
  5.5 Repeating
  5.6 Associating
6 *Interpreting*
  6.1 Explaining
  6.2 Questioning
  6.3 Fantasizing
7 *Informing*
  7.1 Giving information
  7.2 Giving advice
  7.3 Suggestions
	1 *Supporting*
	  1.1 Contacting
	  1.2 Reassuring
	  1.3 Relaxing
	2 *Crisis intervening*
	  2.1 Building hope
	  2.2 Consoling
	  2.3 Controlling
	  2.4 Developing
	     alternatives
	3 *Centering*
	  3.1 Identifying
	     strengths
	  3.2 Reviewing growth
	     experiences
	  3.3 Recalling Peak
	     experiences
	4 *Referring*
		1 *Problem solving and decision-making*
		  1.1 Identifying problems
		  1.2 Changing problems to
		     goals
		  1.3 Analyzing problems
		  1.4 Exploring alternatives
		     and implications
		  1.5 Planning a course of
		     action
		  1.6 Generalizing to new
		     problems
		2 *Behaviour changing*
		  2.1 Modeling
		  2.2 Rewarding
		  2.3 Extinguishing
		  2.4 Desensitizing

Source: Lawrence M. Brammer, *The Helping Relationship: Process and Skills*, 2nd ed., © 1979, p. 19. Reprinted by permission of Prentice-Hall, Inc., Englewood Cliffs, N.J.

Designing and Implementing Action will draw on the interviewer's knowledge of resources, creative and divergent thinking and problem solving skills. Many careers counselling interviews will follow a process similar to the one described in the Egan model, and this perhaps explains the use of this counselling model in careers officer training courses. There will, of course, be occasions during the helping interview when the careers practitioner feels insufficiently skilled or trained to deal adequately with a client's problems. In this case, it is useful to know to whom clients in special difficulties can be referred if the need arises and to have on hand a list of professional agencies and other counselling contacts. Recognizing the limits of one's skills in the helping encounter is particularly important, both in ensuring that clients are helped effectively and in identifying one's own training needs, since the development of counsellor skills and awarenesses is a continuing process without a finite end!

Careers Counselling

Counselling, simply stated, is the helping interview in a more elaborated form and is a term used to describe a process of helping, the central feature of which is an emphasis on learning. For the most part, counselling is concerned with helping people develop both skills and awarenesses to cope with their everyday lives and to anticipate future events and changes. Careers counselling, in comparison with other forms of counselling, is concerned primarily with an individual's career development. Whereas a personal or educational counsellor may be concerned with issues of emotional adjustment or study problems, a careers counsellor is likely to be faced primarily with clients who are making career decisions and choices or coping with life changes which relate to their working life — job change, redundancy, unemployment and so on. It has been argued by Newsome and others (1973) that the distinction between vocational counselling and other forms of counselling is an arbitary one and indeed that careers counselling does not warrant a separate status of its own. The author, however, shares the view of Tyler (1969) that careers counselling practitioners, whether careers and guidance teachers or careers advisers, need to have some background knowledge of the world of work, in particular knowledge of the structure of the occupational system in order to help their clients effectively. This does not mean that careers practitioners need have a detailed knowledge of every occupation, but should at least know in broad terms how one occupational *field*, for example, banking or engineering differs from another and be aware of the different *levels* of jobs within each field. Conventionally the concept of occupational level is expressed in terms of skill and training required, for example, unskilled, semi-skilled, skilled and so on, and each occupational field will have its own particular levels of entry corresponding to the particular occupational level.

A broad knowledge of occupations is essential for careers counselling. For example, in counselling a student who has an overriding ambition to study medicine at a medical school and who, it seems, is unlikely to achieve the necessary qualifications, it will be useful for the counsellor to have some knowledge of hospital and medical careers and the levels of entry and qualifications required. Then, with the sensitive use of alternative suggestions at the planning stage of the interview, the counsellor will be able to enlarge the client's view of the total range of opportunities available, if it is seen by the client that entering medical school is an unattainable goal. A knowledge of both occupational field and level will therefore enable the counsellor to provide reasonable occupational suggestions if the need arises.

It may be useful at this stage to say something of the use of occupational information in careers counselling. As we saw earlier, the helping interview is not the best vehicle for giving information to clients and yet there is often a temptation to feed the client with information rather than concentrate on what the interviewee is really saying. Indeed, the introduction of vast amounts of occupational facts during the interview may only serve to obscure the student's real needs and confuse the relationship between counsellor and client. The main aim of the counsellor will be to help the client to define his or her own information needs, to point out where the information can be found and to show the client how the information can be used. If information is introduced during the counselling interview, it is probably best done by allowing the client to read the material; then an opportunity can be provided for the client to comment on and say how he/she feels about the information that the counsellor has introduced. According to Tyler (1969),

> ' . . . it wastes the time of counsellor and client to spend any part of the initial interview, potentially valuable for bringing out subtle attitudes, in discussing facts that may or may not have some bearing on the problems.'

Often a request for information on the client's part may be no more than an initial starting point for discussion and can be simply seen as a 'presenting' issue. The presenting issue or problem is often used by the client to test the ground in the helping interview and to see whether he or she is able to trust the counsellor with other, perhaps more sensitive issues. The A-level student who suddenly announces to the sixth form tutor or careers officer that she has decided not to take up her place on a degree course may during the course of the helping interview reveal that her real worry is about the financial burden it might impose on her parents who may be experiencing financial difficulties. After the exploration phase of the interview is completed, it may then be possible for the counsellor to introduce positive suggestions concerned with issues such as covenanting which may make the financial situation easier or enable the student to see that the grant system is flexible enough to take into account any sudden drop in parental income. Whatever the outcome of the interview, the interviewer who is sensitive to the idea of the presenting problem will be able to help the client explore all the aspects of the problem. Similarly, the final year student who seeks help with deciding what to do on graduation, presenting the question, 'What shall I do when I leave?', may be genuinely seeking help with career decision-making. On the other hand, the student may reveal during the course of the interview that he has plenty of ideas and opportunities for work, but feels considerable pressure from parents and peers to go out and get a 'proper career' rather than take some form of enjoyable temporary work which may provide valuable experience.

It is not always easy to recognize whether what is being presented is what constitutes the client's real concerns. Attending closely to clients' physical appearance, body language and tone of voice may well provide useful clues. If the client's tone of voice is inappropriate to the content of what he or she is saying, if the client continually uses 'oughts' and 'shoulds' in describing plans, if he or she has largely negative responses to make about suggestions for action, it may be likely that there are other matters on the 'agenda' and it will be up to the counsellor to renegotiate the starting point for the interview.

The Use of Test Data

Although not widely used in this country, some careers counsellors may want to introduce the use of interest or aptitude tests in their counselling interviews, particularly as part of the process of self-exploration and identification of interests which is characteristic of so many career choice and decision-making interviews. The idea of taking a test of some kind may be that of the counsellor or indeed the client, but however the idea originated, the rationale for the testing will need careful explanation and the way in which the results are introduced into the interview will require skilful and sensitive handling. There are some guidelines for the introduction of test results in the counselling interview. Before talking about the test results, it is often valuable to let the client talk about his or her response to the test itself and to describe how he or she felt about the test items and how he or she coped. The client should be given the test data in its simplest form and be given a chance to put his or her own interpretation on the results and to look at the implications for a career decision.

It is possible for the counsellor to remain neutral to the results of the test and at the same time, with sensitive attending and leading, encourage the client's own self-evaluation. From a counselling perspective, the test data will be useful only in as much as they help the client to learn something new about him/herself, and the counsellor may do well to avoid too much interpretation. For the more the counsellor interprets the results, the more likely it is that the helping interview will resemble a diagnostic guidance and advice giving interview and the less the client will feel able to make his or her own decisions. With the use of aptitude and intelligence tests, in particular, it will be important for the counsellor to be prepared for any defensive reactions on the client's part, when test results run counter to the client's own expectations.

The same general pointers can be used when discussing the results of computer-based careers guidance systems. Rather than use the information on the computer printout as a diagnostic predictor, it will be up to counsellor and client jointly to evaluate the occupational suggestions and integrate the results within a decision-making framework.

The Counselling Relationship

Most definitions of counselling emphasize the need for counselling to be a continuing process between counsellor and client rather than a once and for all encounter. The continuing success of this process will consequently depend on the relationship that is established between counsellor and client, interviewer and interviewee. Careers officers and careers advisers dealing predominantly with vocational counselling and faced with heavy caseloads may view this aspect of the counselling process with some scepticism and ask how can they afford the luxury of building successful counselling relationships with their clients, when faced with a continual stream of new clients. Nevertheless, the qualities and counsellor competencies required for the establishment of a successful relationship between counsellor and client are relevant to any helping interview and require some elaboration.

A good deal has been written about the qualities needed to be a successful helper and counsellor and there appears to be some consensus on the need for the helper to show empathy, to be an effective communicator and to be aware of one's own self and values and how these might help or hinder the helping relationship. The three essential characteristics of the successful helper have been variously summarized by Tyler (1969) as Understanding, Acceptance and Sincerity and by Rogers (1957) as Empathetic Understanding, Unconditional Positive Regard and Congruence (see Figure 3.4).

Figure 3.4. Counsellor Attributes

Rogers	Tyler
Empathetic understanding	Understanding
Unconditional positive regard	Acceptance
Congruence	Sincerity

Source: Rogers (1957) and Tyler (1969).

Understanding

One of the primary qualities necessary for a successful helping encounter is that of understanding or empathy — being able to stand in another person's shoes and share and enter into their world. Obviously sympathetic responses, such as, 'Oh, I'm so sorry to hear that you've lost your job', say more about the feelings of the person talking than revealing understanding of how the interviewee or client sees the jobless situation. Sympathy is not the same as empathy. By attending carefully, the interviewer or counsellor understands by listening carefully and perceiving everything the client is trying to say and share the client's frame of reference. According to Gilmore (1973), the process of understanding can be likened to that of appreciating an impressionist painting. It is not characterized by a search for detailed facts or information, but relies on a generalized sense or impression of the client's situation.

Acceptance

Whereas understanding has to do with the way an interviewer or counsellor *thinks* about the client's situation, acceptance is to do with the way a counsellor *feels*. It implies that whoever the client might be, the counsellor will exhibit a caring manner and give his whole time and complete attention. Counsellors will therefore be tolerant of clients whose values differ from their own. According to Gilmore, acceptance in counselling 'is the celebration of diversity and complexity in others' and it is to do with liking, respecting, appreciating and being genuinely interested in the interviewee. Acceptance is not helped by cynicism, impatience or blocking responses, such as, 'when I was your age things were different!' It is certainly not encouraged by interviewers who try to reinforce their positions of status and who talk down to the client rather than work on the basis of equal sharing. To be truly accepting of a client, it is important for the counsellor to be aware of his or her own values, biases and prejudices.

Sincerity

The third attribute which is important in the establishment of the counselling encounter is that of sincerity or the capacity to respond in a genuine or authentic way. It will be helpful to the client to know that the counsellor is taking him seriously and will act as an 'honest broker' in resolving problems and that there is no 'hidden' agenda to the interview, for example. Intricately linked with the quality of sincerity in the counselling interview are notions of confidentiality and trust. One of the ground rules of any helping encounter is that whatever the client divulges in the interview remains confidential to counsellor and client and may only be revealed elsewhere with the client's consent.

The notion of sincerity may pose particular problems for counsellors who see themselves as principally system oriented (Law, 1978) as opposed to client oriented. If the counsellor feels, for example, that a student 'ought' to remain in his school or college to take the A-level course to keep up the student numbers, this hidden agenda for the counselling interview will work against the development of sincerity in the counselling relationship if it is not acknowledged by the counsellor and made known to the client.

Approaches to Careers Counselling

As Daws (1976) points out, the major influence on counselling practice in this country has been that of student or client centred counselling and the work of Carl Rogers. This is particularly so of personal and educational counsellors, whose work has focused on the personal growth of their clients and who view counselling as a process which is essentially person rather than problem centred. As far as careers counselling is concerned, however, developmental and behavioural perspectives has enjoyed equal importance since, arguably, the two principal questions faced by careers counsellors in their work, are, firstly, 'At what stage are my clients in their career development?' and secondly, 'What skills do they need to learn to develop their career further in starting work, changing job and so on?' The questions are important because they both illustrate different approaches to careers counselling and suggest different theoretical perspectives to the careers counselling interview.

Careers teachers and careers officers experienced in interviewing and adolescents will be all too aware of the number of times young people mention working with children or horses or becoming an airline pilot as their expressed career intention. According to Super (1957), this is natural of the Exploration stage of career development, when adolescents work through their phantasy ideas towards greater realism in their job and career choice. Likewise, Ginzberg (1951) sees the period of early adolescence (ages 11–17) as the Tentative stage of career development when students begin to gain a greater awareness of their own interests, abilities and values. A developmental perspective is therefore useful for the process of careers counselling. It helps to explain why some students are more able to make a commitment to vocational training than others, why some students will hold on for some considerable time to career goals which are clearly unattainable and why, for example, students graduating in their mid-20s may feel considerable pressure to settle in a particular occupational field as they approach the Establishment stage of the career development process.

Indeed, for Healey (1982) all careers counselling interventions need to be related to a particular career development stage and will vary to some extent according to the age of the client. During the Growth stage (age 14) he argues that the primary emphasis will be on self-awareness counselling since pupils and students will still be a long way from the prospect of work entry. During the Exploratory stage (ages 15–24) of career development, careers counselling will be as much concerned with educational choices and their vocational implications as with career decision-making. The kind of counselling interview will depend on where the client is on the continuum of education, training and work entry. Placement counselling will also be a feature of this stage of development, as will counselling concerned with work adjustment and transition. During the Establishment stage, the focus for careers counselling will be the broad one of career and life planning, and be more likely to take account of family and long-term relationships in the client's personal and career development.

As we saw in an earlier chapter, American writers have often linked a developmental perspective to the concept of career maturity, and while there is a considerable American literature and research on the concept of career maturity, little emphasis in this country has been given to the idea that it may be possible to identify the stage of development reached by the client prior to or during the careers counselling interview. It may, however, be useful for careers practitioners to use the kind of framework provided by a career maturity model like that of Crites (shown in Figure 3.5). In this case the career maturity of adolescents can be defined against four factors:

Figure 3.5. A Model of Career Maturity in Adolescence

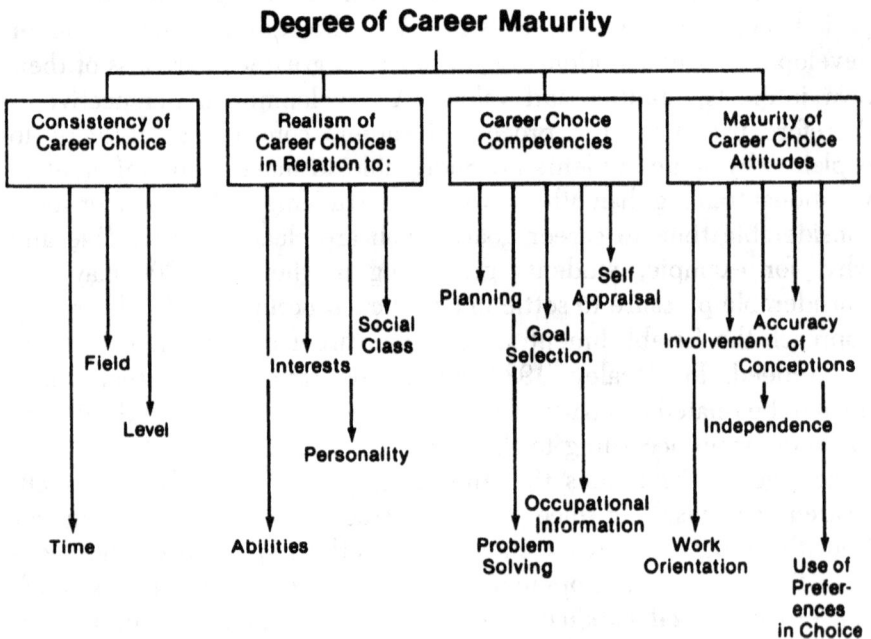

1   consistency of career choice;
2   realism of choices;
3   competencies in choice and decision-making; and
4   maturity of attitude.

Central to the concept of career maturity is that clients should possess sufficient choice and decision-making competencies to proceed to later stages of their career development. The question is then raised how careers practitioners can help their clients improve their skills in choices and decisions as part of the counselling process. It is in this particular context that behavioural counselling, with its emphasis on skill development and goal setting through reinforcement and modelling, has had a particular impact on careers counselling practice. In particular, Krumboltz and Thoreson (1976) have gone some way to show that career decision-making, like any other problem solving behaviour, is a question of setting and finding ways of achieving appropriate goals. In helping clients with the question, 'What career should I choose?', the counsellor should provide an appropriate plan for clients, which will enable them to use a systematic process to move to a career decision. By *determining* the problem, *exploring* the alternatives, *clarifying* values, *seeking* out information and looking at the implications of various courses of action and *eliminating* the least likely alternatives, clients can learn about the process of decision-making itself, which they can then use in other areas of their lives rather than on making the right career decision. According to Krumboltz and Baker (1973):

> The initial goal of the behavioural counsellor is to assist the vocationally undecided client to achieve his stated objective of a suitable vocational choice; and, at the same time, to accomplish one of the major aims of counselling, helping the client to become a wise decision maker. A wise decision maker is one who maximizes his chances for making a successful choice by engaging in forethoughtful planning and problem solving. How the client makes a decision is the focal point of the counsellor's efforts. What the client decides is his own concern based upon his personal values and goals.

The technique of behavioural counselling can be helpful in many of the issues presented to careers counsellors. A common example, that of modelling, can be used in helping clients who are having difficulties in coping successfully with a job selection interview and takes the form of a 'mock' selection interview between counsellor and client. Firstly, the careers counsellor takes on the role of an *interviewee* in a role play of a selection interview, with the client asking the questions and taking the employer's role. During the role play it will be possible for the counsellor to model or illustrate the most appropriate replies and responses to questions and hence give the client an idea of the most appropriate way of handling a job interview. The roles can then be reversed and the client can rehearse the role of interviewee using the appropriate styles of response. A review of several theoretical approaches to the careers counselling process is provided by Crites (1981).

Whilst much of the previous discussion has centred on the helping interview and the *process* of careers counselling, the following checklist is intended to give some idea of the *content* of careers counselling interviews and the kinds of issues and problems which are presented during an interview. The six problem areas:

uncertainty over course choice;
inability to make a career decision;
feeling blocked in career development;
coping with redundancy or unemployment;
loss of confidence and fear of rejection in making job applications,

are those which are most commonly presented.

Uncertainty over Course Choice

Themes which are likely to be explored:

previous educational experiences, the client's successes and failures;
the client's academic and vocational interests and values;
personal learning style and course assessment methods;
the social milieu of the course, the kinds of tutors and students;
the vocational outcomes of the course and the career development implications of completing the course successfully.

Inability to Make a Career Decision

Themes which are likely to be explored:

the client's previous decision-making styles;
the awareness and clarification of interests and values, skills and abilities;

the depth and extent of information available about different alternatives;

feeling of confidence, or lack of it, about personal potential;

the recognition of real or imaginary blocks and barriers to implementing ideas;

conflict in family or relationships over the client's ideas.

Feeling Blocked in Career Development

Themes which are likely to be explored:

relationships with superiors at place of work;
changing career aspirations or life style considerations;
coping with feelings of boredom and depression;
questioning of present qualification level and training;
managing attempts to change routines and increase job variety;
examining feelings of the need for recognition and reward.

Coping with Redundancy or Unemployment

Themes which are likely to be explored:

coming to terms with loss of status and work identity;
recognizing feelings of anger and depression;
ways of coping with increased time to oneself;
identifying personal resources and useful support groups and agencies;
coping with isolation and aloneness.

Loss of Confidence and Fear of Rejection in Making Job Applications

having to cope with loss of self-worth and self-esteem after each rejection;

coping with the inability to discover the reasons for rejection;

maintaining the momentum of job search and sense of planfulness;

coping with feelings of increasing uncertainty about the future;

allowing oneself to be side-tracked by other safer and more enjoyable activities.

71

Evaluation

A major problem in evaluating the careers counselling process is in deciding whether to focus on the counselling process itself — what the client learns from the interview — or on the outcome of counselling in terms of success at work, job finding, etc. In the past, many of the British evaluations of the careers interview have focused primarily on interview outcomes and have sought to establish whether the careers adviser's suggestions and recommendations have led to greater occupational satisfaction or success on the part of the client. Cherry (1974) found that there was a relationship between the careers officer's suggestions at interview and the length of time spent by young people in their first jobs. An emphasis on interview outcomes naturally tends to reinforce the view of occupational choice as a once and for all process and interviewing as part of a basic matching process, particularly if the outcome is seen solely in terms of jobs, rather than the learning outcomes — greater self-awareness, decision-making ability and so on.

More recently, Lloyd and Wilson (1980) asked recipients of fifth year careers officer interviews to judge the interviewer's effectiveness. The results showed generally that students had mixed set of expectations of the careers interview, but that 62.4 per cent found the interview very useful, 35.5 per cent said it was fairly useful and 19 per cent not very useful. In answer to the question, 'What did you think was the main purpose of the interview', 20 per cent saw it in terms of help with career or course choice, 33.4 as an opportunity for information giving and 19.7 as a chance for the careers officer to get to know about them. The spread of responses to this question suggests that the fifth year careers interview carried out on a blanket basis lacked a single clearly defined purpose, but tended towards information giving and screening of career intentions.

A more rigorous study by Coolbear and Fairbairns (1981) of the work of the Centre for Professional and Executive Career Development and Counselling (CEPEC) provides interesting evaluation of the outcomes of careers counselling. One hundred unemployed people, from the PER register, mainly male and in mid-career, had access to careers counselling over a four-month period. A separate comparison group that did not attend for counselling was matched with the experimental group in terms of age, length of time unemployed and occupational group.

The results showed that those who attended for careers counselling found new employment faster than the control group, were more active in their job search and given more interviews, even though at the end of the process the comparison groups had found a similar number of jobs.

Eighty per cent of respondents said they had found the experience of counselling useful, mentioning particularly their improved morale and confidence, greater sense of direction and increased ability to market themselves.

Whilst the study focused primarily on the job search outcomes of the counselling process, it is clear that those taking part benefited from the counselling they received and in some cases, clients reported improved interpersonal relationships and ability to cope with work stress. Additionally, a number of case studies reported improved personal appearance, increased confidence and release from depression for those who had taken part in the experimental group, half of whom had been unemployed for over a year. It seems clear from this study that when careers counselling is seen as a process over a given time span, real learning and change can result.

For the most part, this chapter has focused on the use of the helping interview in careers work as a way of helping individuals in their career development. One of the principal assumptions underlying the use of the helping interview is that clients and students will refer themselves for interviewing and counselling, rather than be obliged to attend as part of a screening process or 'blanket approach' which characterizes many school-based careers interviews. Often as part of a guidance programme, careers practitioners may feel the need to carry out other kinds of interview, perhaps to do with information gathering or screening. Essentially, this latter kind of interview is largely system oriented — it enables the careers practitioner to gather information for the need of the school or careers service, rather than focus primarily on the needs of the interviewee. In this kind of interview, the skills described earlier of active listening, attending and open questioning will still be appropriate, as they will during placement interviews. As research has shown, however, for the interview to be effective, the first requirement is that the reason and rationale for the interview should be fully understood by the client taking part.

Chapter 4

Aids to Career Decision-Making

The careers education and counselling approaches outlined in previous chapters lay particular emphasis on the process of career decision-making and the ability of individuals to effect choices and decisions for themselves. Some writers, Gelatt (1962), Tiedman and O'Hara (1963), have made decision-making the central focus for their theories of career development. The assumption underlying these approaches is that clients can make career decisions successfully for themselves and that helping professionals can aid an individual gain self-understanding, assimilate appropriate careers information and effect choices, with the emphasis not on making wise decisions but on making decisions wisely (Katz, 1969). Instead of becoming the passive recipient of expert advice, in a career planning and counselling model the client is enabled to function proactively and work at decisions for him or herself. A further assumption underlying the focus in careers decision-making is that, once learned, the approach and skills can be employed throughout one's personal and career development.

Most career decisions imply a sifting through and synthesis of information, firstly about *SELF*, and secondly about the *OPPORTUNITIES* that are available or can be created. The aim of this chapter is concerned with the aids that are used in careers work to achieve this synthesis between clients and their ideas about possible futures. It concentrates on three different kinds of stimulus to career decision-making — careers information, which provides information about opportunities; occupational interest guides, which encourage an awareness of self; and computer-based programmes, which provide feedback about self in relation to different kinds of opportunity and career area.

A Model for Career Decision-Making

It is now generally accepted amongst careers practitioners that career decision-making involves a series of decisions over a life span, rather than one single once and for all decision. It can be seen as an ongoing process, in which choices are reversible, and changes in circumstances, opportunities or personal values may bring about the need for new decisions. The way individuals approach career and life decisions and the meaning they ascribe to life events is a less clearly researched topic and yet seems important in understanding the career decision-making process. Arroba (1977) has distinguished six decision-making styles employed by people describing their life decisions:

> *Logical*, in which choices are rationally and systematically appraised;
>
> *Hesitant*, in which a delaying tactic or procrastination has a dominant feature;
>
> *Emotional*, implying the use of entirely subjective preferences and feelings;
>
> *Intuitive*, with an emphasis on personal feelings of 'rightness' or inevitability;
>
> *Compliant*, a passive style, in which events or circumstances or perceived expectations tend to determine the decision;
>
> *No thought*, included in this category are rapid, impulsive decisions and those which routinely encountered, may be seen to require little preparation.

In her conclusion, Arroba points out that decision-making style may be as much a function of how the decider perceives a given situation as of personal characteristics. In other words, we may use different decision-making styles according to circumstance. From a career planning point of view, most American writers argue that career decisions can be made in a rational and logical manner if the client:

> understands the decision-making process;
> makes decisions based on self-knowledge;
> uses relevant career or occupational information;
> can evaluate the alternative courses of action and their consequences.

These four stages or characteristics of logical decision-making styles are the basis of a number of systematic approaches (Gelatt, 1962). The DECIDES mnemonic described in Figure 4.1 developed by Krumbolz (1977) provides a very useful framework for inclusion in careers education programmes, emphasizing as it does a skill-based, behavioural approach to career decision-making and the teaching of career decision-making skills.

It also encourages clients to seek and evaluate information in an

Figure 4.1.   A Model for Career Decision-Making.

Career decision-making

Action plan for _____*Paul*_____   Today's date: _____*Sept. 15*_____

Steps	Actions	Completion Date

1 Define the problem
Name at least one possible job related to my
interests and abilities   *Sept. 15*

2 Establish an action plan   *Sept. 15*

3 Clarify values
a. Talk with friends, parents, and other people
    about what's important in a career   *Sept. 25*
b. Take part in some values clarification exercises
c. Write a statement of what's important to me

4 Identify alternatives
a. Take an interest inventory   *Oct. 10*
b. Use job-screening system
c. Consult books and pamphlets about jobs
d. Take an aptitude test battery
e. List jobs I've already done successfully

5 Discover probable outcomes
a. Explore job simulation experiences   *Nov. 5*
b. Talk with people employed in occupations that
    I'm considering
c. Read descriptions of occupations
d. Estimate my chances for success in each job
e. Judge how well each job fits my values

6 Eliminate alternatives systematically
a. Delete least feasible alternatives   *Nov. 10*
b. Explore remaining alternatives more thoroughly

7 Start action
Begin investigating possible training opportunities or
listing potential employers   *Nov. 15*

Source: Reprinted with permission from *Guide to Career Decision-Making Skills*.
Copyright © 1977 by College Entrance Examination Board, New York.

active and positive way, to commit a given amount of time to each stage of the process and can be applied equally well to other life decisions. As a model, it can incorporate many of the measures described in this chapter — interest guides and computer-based careers guidance systems — and can therefore provide an approach to which both careers practitioners and clients can work. This systematic approach implies that the process of careers information begins with the setting of a goal, for example, 'I'm going to decide what to do when I leave school', which is then followed by a process of trying to increase self-awareness and it is only then that detailed occupational information will be necessary. For those floundering over a career decision, precise occupational information is often the last thing they may need, although it may be seen as a safe starting point for discussion with a careers specialist.

The Role of Careers Information

Having access to relevant, up to date, occupational information is an essential part of the career decision-making process. The last ten years have seen a considerable expansion in the availability of careers information, both in the amount that is published each year by publishing houses and in the provision of careers resource centres and information rooms in schools, colleges and careers offices. Alongside this expansion, a change has also occurred in the way careers information is used. It is no longer stored solely for the careers adviser's benefit, but made openly accessible to clients to aid their decision-making, with careers information staff sharing with careers counsellors a far greater sense of client centredness in their work. Careers resource centres and information rooms are therefore tailored specifically to meet the needs of a particular client group. Schools, colleges, polytechnics and universities will all have information facilities geared to the needs of their client group. There is a growing literature on the design and functioning of careers information rooms and on the processes of accessing and classifying information from employers, training boards and professional bodies in an ever increasing variety of formats: printed brochures, books and video. Many of these topics are ably covered by Isaacson (1977).

Careers information is likely to come from a variety of sources and take a number of different forms (see Figure 4.2). Generally speaking, occupational information which describes a particular occupational group (such as banking or insurance) is readily available. Labour market information, on the other hand, which predicts the number of bank trainees recruited annually, is not widely available in this country. We

Figure 4.2.   Careers Information: A Typology

Nature of information

LABOUR MARKET DATA
Information on employers
Manpower forecasts
Employment trends
Recruitment advertizing

OCCUPATIONAL INFORMATION
Occupational literature
    showing education and training
    requirements
Course compendia
Information from
    professional bodies
    and training boards

LIFE STYLE INFORMATION
Job/case studies on
    individuals at work
Interviews with working
    people
Attitude questionnaires
    and surveys
Press/magazine/television
    features

have no real equivalent to the *Occupational Outlook Handbook*, which predicts annually the demand for different kinds of labour in the United States of America. Equally, information concerning the total life style of certain occupations is only gradually taking on an increasing significance. Our concern here is to determine the kind of occupational information which is most useful in the career decision-making process. In a detailed study, Hayes (1971) examined the place of occupational information in the process of occupational choice, adjustment to work and the development of worker identities. He was able to distinguish, after appraising the literature on job satisfaction and occupational information, eight major categories for careers information.

1   Entry requirements and job demands.
2   Content and nature of work.
3   Administrative work situation.

4   Social work situation.
5   Physical work environment.
6   Information of long-term relevance (career development implications).
7   Organizational, occupational and product image.
8   Global life style implications.

Hayes found that prior to work entry, young workers considered the economic aspects of the job to be the most important, that is, details of the immediate job demands and nature of the work itself. After a period of work experience, however, the psycho-social aspects of the work situation increased significantly in importance. His findings led him to conclude that there exists 'a pressing need to present and communicate a range of information which accurately reflects the full reality of occupations, including their economic and psychosocial aspects.'

Despite the recent expansion in careers information provision in schools, careers offices and higher education, much of the information is still concerned with the 'economic' aspects highlighted by Hayes, and slow progress has been made in assembling information concerning life style as well as information which is specific to jobs. Understandably, it is far easier for careers teachers and careers information officers to assemble information which relates to large organizations, such as the civil service, with well defined entry points, selection procedures and abundant careers literature, than it is to provide information on the life style implications of running a small business. It is, however, clear that much of the psycho-social information necessary for career decision-making can be gained from initiatives outside the careers information centre, in particular from work experience placements and job study visits which encourage clients to seek information for themselves in preparation for their choice of occupational role.

Initiatives in community guidance may therefore make up for any deficiencies in published careers information. A work experience placement organized in a hospital ward, for example, may well provide a client with a far clearer idea of the reality of nursing as a career than an occupational leaflet. One can evaluate a range of information sources according to the extent to which they provide a realistic picture of what it's like to perform certain kinds of work.

According to Kunze's model (Figure 4.3), there is a spectrum of occupational information provision which can be provided in a number of different methods. The most direct way of gaining information is by work experience and work sampling, which will include the psycho-social factors mentioned earlier. At the other end of the spectrum,

Figure 4.3.   *Spectrum of Occupational Information*

Extent of directness	Classification	Characteristics
10	Work experience on the job	Provide direct contact with
9	Work sampling	actual work situations
8	Direct observations — visiting work settings	
7	Experience in simulated environments, for example, training workshops	Simulation of work settings and occupational roles
6	Simulations, games and role play	
5	Interviews with experts or representatives of occupations	Information is processed by and adapted to the needs of
4	Computer-based systems	the individual
3	Programmed instructional materials, such as workbooks	
2	Audio visual aids, video film, etc.	Information is post method,
1	Publications: books, information sheets and articles	fixed and designed for general use

Source: Adapted from K. Kunze (1967) 'Industry resources available to counsellors', *Vocational Guidance Quarterly*, 16, p. 138.
Copyright (1967) American Personnel and Guidance Association. Reprinted with permission.

printed information in books, information sheets and articles is of necessity going to provide information of the least direct and most generalized kind.

It will be clear from this analysis that providing careers information in printed form is effective, but at a basic level, in providing information about training routes, entry qualifications, job requirements and so on. Opportunities for work sampling, job studies and even classroom simulation and role play may then be able to convey to a student what it is really like to do a particular job and thus provide a firmer basis for career decision.

Decision-Making and Self-Awareness

In most career choice and decision-making models the primary focus is on encouraging the client's self-awareness. Only when the student or client has a realistic sense of his or her own abilities, skills, values and interests will he or she be able to make some kind of decision about the future. In terms of the DECIDES mnemonic mentioned earlier, for example, careers and occupational information is seen as important during later stages of the decision-making process. The first steps are concerned with clarifying values and interests.

In careers work in this country little attention has been paid to the influence of occupational values on career development and yet there is considerable American research evidence to suggest that values play a large part in determining occupational choice and attainment. Osipow (1973) cites a number of studies showing this relationship. In particular, it seems that values play an important part in course choice. Students on education and social work courses have as their highest value working with people in a helping manner; architecture, drama and art students, perhaps not surprisingly, value self-expression more than other groups; business and management students value money, social status and prestige. In the American literature on career development values identification is seen as one of the major components of the careers counselling and careers education process. In this country, on the other hand, the primary focus has been on occupational interests with careers practitioners concerning themselves with the question, 'What are you interested in?' rather than 'What do you value?'

Occupational Interest Guides

Tests and measures of occupational interest have been a central feature of careers guidance work in this country, particularly in local authority careers services. Their use and development owes much to the diagnostic models of vocational guidance outlined in previous chapters and like other measures of psychometric assessment they have been designed to provide careers advisers with objective assessment measures which claim statistical validity and reliability. The use of tests in a counselling context is well documented in Goldman (1971) and the use of tests in British careers work is summarized by Holdsworth and Clarke (1980c). The aim of this chapter is to show how test results can be an aid to career decision-making and to affirm that in educational and vocational counselling the main rationale for the use of tests is to assist a client in achieving greater clarification of his or her self-concept. It is important to distinguish between tests of ability and aptitudes, for example, Morrisby Differential Test Battery and Department of Employment Vocational Assessment Tests, which are used primarily for diagnostic guidance purposes, and measures of occupational interest which can be used more readily by the clients themselves, without lengthy interpretation by a qualified psychometrician.

Perhaps the most widely used occupational interest guide in this country has been the APU (Applied Psychology Unit) devised by Closs at the University of Edinburgh. Work on the guide started in 1966 and after several intermediate versions the latest edition now forms part of the JIIG-CAL computerized guidance system described below.

Two particular features have been common to each successive version of the APU guide: its reliance on paired comparisons (asking users to choose between two matched items) in the structure of the guide and on scoring which is ipsative rather than normative. In very simple terms, the latest version of the guide assumes that there are six separate areas of occupational interest and to provide a pattern for a client's interests, statements of job activities representing those six basic areas are matched against each other.

For example,
Dismantle and repair cameras .... A
Identify chemicals in samples of soil .... B

Clients are asked to make a final choice and state a preference for one of the two items, both of which have been chosen because of their equal weightings (the population sample used in the test construction found them equally attractive). This method of matching items in pairs is known to psychometricians as the method of paired comparisons. By inviting clients to do this successively (in the current version sixty paired comparisons are presented) it is possible to build a profile of the client's preferred occupational interests over the six areas:

Type 1 Making and repairing things where you need to be good with your hands. Using tools for drilling, sawing, welding, etc. to make things. Assembling parts to make machines or repairing them. Installing plumbing and electrical wiring. Doing work on buildings or houses.

Type 2 Work where you have to know how to look after living things. Knowing about different kinds of animals, what food they need and how to keep them healthy. Knowing about plants and how to grow them. Harvesting crops. Working on farms and with wild animals and plants too.

Type 3 Clerical and sales work where you need to be able to count, add money and help with bookkeeping. Typing letters and bills. Giving tickets and making bookings. Demonstrating and selling things.

Type 4   Work where neatness and an eye for colour and shape are important. Making things out of leather, cloth, wood and other craft materials. Painting things, decorating them and arranging them to look nice. Cooking, baking and making food look attractive.

Type 5   Giving practical help to people in need. Helping to nurse patients. Protecting people and rescuing them from danger. Helping those injured in accidents. Visiting old people. Looking after small children, reading them stories, playing with them and showing them how to make and do things.

Type 6   Work where you have to be good at being friendly and chatting to people. Meeting people and making them welcome. Showing them round places and pointing things out to them. Entertaining them. Giving information, advice, demonstrations and making announcements.

The other unique feature of the guide is its choice in ipsative scoring, and it is on this issue that Closs has parted company with the conventional orthodoxy surrounding the construction of psychological measures. In most tests of aptitude or personality, a client's score or profile is usually measured against a population norm, to make it standardized and 'objective'. In the construction of the APU Closs has rejected the idea of normative scoring, arguing that it is more important for a client's profile to be internally consistent with itself, and to fully reflect the nature of a particular client's interests, a process called *ipsative* scoring. Hence, in the example provided above,

Dismantle and repair cameras .... A
Identify chemicals in samples of soil .... B

clients completing the guide not only have to make a choice between two statements, but also have to say whether they like, dislike or are indifferent to each of the statements. In scoring the guide it is then clear whether clients have completed the questionnaire on a logically consistent form, in other words that their preference scores are matched by their like/dislike statements.

Like the JIIG-CAL system, of which it forms part, the APU guide enjoys two important advantages which are not usually found in other occupational interest guides. Firstly, it is divided into six sections according to the level of training/academic qualifications usually necessary to perform the job activities described. This means in practice that the client can choose to consider activities at any particular occupational level and at the same time makes it an appropriate tool for any secondary school or further education student (see Figure 4.4).

Figure 4.4. Sections of the JIIG-CAL System

Section	Qualifications	Training	Study needed?	Section
A	None needed	Up to about 3 months	No	A
B	Not usually needed but some passes might help	2–3 months	No, not usually	B
C	Os or CSEs often asked for but you could still get some jobs without them	About 2–4 years	Yes, part of the training usually means going to college — say 1 day a week	C
D	A number of Os would be essential	About 3–5 years	Yes, study (full-time or part-time) usually quite important	D
E	As or Hs would be needed in relevant subjects	About 3–5 years	Yes, full-time study often forms part of the training	E
F	2–3 As or 3–4 Hs plus Os required. Good grades in main subjects often necessary	About 4–5 years. Sometimes 6 or more years	Yes, you would normally need a degree or an equivalent qualification	F

Source: S.J. Closs (1983) *JIIG-CAL Information Booklet*, Release III. Reproduced by permission of the author.

Secondly, Closs has designed this version of the guide to be used by clients for themselves as a means of stimulating self-assessment rather than to produce results which remain part of a careers practitioner's diagnostic equipment. The aim is not to provide a method of assessment for use by teachers but to aid a student's decision-making. With the emphasis on JIIG-CAL being used as a complete component of a careers education programme (described in more detail below) it is clear that the APU and the entire system is a genuine attempt to synthesize information about *self* and about *opportunities* and hence will enable clients to progress towards a more concrete self-image at the same time as they are learning about different occupations and their suitability for them.

The Crowley Occupational Interests Blank is another widely used interest questionnaire. Designed specifically for the average and below-average ability school pupil, it does not claim to be an objective test or measure of occupational interests, but a simple measure of the overall direction of a person's occupational interests, to be used as a basis for group discussion or individual counselling with third, fourth or fifth year pupils.

Its first part consists of job titles from five different interest areas, which students are asked to place in preference order, for example:

Farm worker	(Active/Outdoor)
Filing clerk	(Office)
Youth club leader	(Social)
Electrician or toy-maker	(Practical)
Hairstylist	(Artistic)

Raw scores are then translated to grades (based on population norms) to provide a profile of interests, for example:

A/O	OFF	SOC	PRA	ART
A	E	C	C+	C

The second part of the guide consists of paired statements about intrinsic occupational satisfactions from which clients are asked to make a forced choice, for example:

The starting pay is good	(Financial gain)
I work regular hours	(Stability/security)
I never have to work alone	(Companionship)
I work in very pleasant surroundings	(Working conditions)
It's the type of work I like	(Interests)

Responses from forty such paired statements then provide a profile of the relative importance to the client of each occupational satisfaction. From the careers specialist's point of view, the interests blank is quick and easy to adminster (it can be administered and marked in one school period) and provides a useful component at an early stage of a school careers programme. It can also be used as a basis for group discussion about job families and occupational groupings. In interpreting the results several points need to be borne in mind. Because the first part of the guide relies on the use of job titles, for example, 'Farm worker', rather than job activities, there is a danger that students will respond simply to the occupational stereotypes, rather than the intrinsic nature of the work, and hence introduce an element of distortion in the results. Secondly, as with all occupational interest guides, there is a likelihood that some students will form 'best impression' sets, that is, they will want to produce the right answer and give a good impression of themselves rather than answer honestly. As Crowley (1976) himself points out, when used in interview, the results always need to be related to other factors, such as educational attainment and subject interests. There may well be some mismatch, for example, between an inventoried interest in *artistic* work and school performance in creative subjects.

Finally, it is important to prevent students drawing incorrect inferences from the results by explaining something of the nature of occupational interests. Questions such as, 'Does this mean I won't be any good at office work?', may well suggest a basic confusion on the client's part about the aims of the interest guide and its predictive nature. Equally, assumptions are frequently made about a 'high' interest score and an individual's suitability for certain kinds of work. It is a common assumption for school pupils, for example, to think that a high *social* score automatically means that a career in social work is their most suitable option. It is clear, therefore, that the interests blank is suited for use as a counselling tool, which needs to be used with the client as part of a careers counselling interview, rather than it being left for clients or students to draw their own conclusions from their interest profiles.

The Self-Directed Search

One measure of occupational interests which has been specifically designed for clients to use by themselves without reference to a vocational counsellor is John Holland's 'Self-Directed Search'. Based on Holland's six-fold classification of personality and working environment outlined in a previous chapter, the questionnaire and the assumptions which underpin it have many characteristics in common with the Vocational Preference Inventory — a personality inventory which is used as a more conventional diagnostic tool.

The Self-Directed Search is a self-administered, self-scored and self-interpreted vocational counselling tool. It consists of a question-naire booklet and a separate 'Occupation Finder', an index of 500 job titles. Clients are first asked to complete the question name booklet which elicits clients' statements about Occupational Daydreams, Job Activities, Personal Competencies, Job Titles, and Self-Estimates of skills and abilities. Each of these statements is then scored against the six-fold classification.

Realistic

The Realistic (R) type likes realistic jobs such as automobile mechanic, aircraft controller, surveyor, farmer, electrician. Has mechanical abilities, but may lack social skills. Is described as:

Conforming	Materialistic	Modest
Frank	Natural	Shy
Honest	Persistent	Stable
Humble	Practical	Thrifty

Investigative

The Investigative (I) types like investigative jobs such as biologist, Chemist, physicist, anthropologist, geologist, medical technologist. Has mathematical and scientific ability but often lacks leadership ability. Is described as:

Analytical	Independent	Modest
Cautious	Intellectual	Precise
Critical	Introverted	Rational
Curious	Methodical	Reserved

Artistic

The Artistic (A) type likes artistic jobs such as composer, musician, stage director, writer, interior decorator, actor/actress. Artistic abilities: writing, musical, or artistic, but often lacks clerical skills. Is described as:

Complicated	Idealistic	Independent
Disorderly	Imaginative	Intuitive
Emotional	Impractical	Nonconforming
Expressive	Impulsive	Original

Social

The Social (S) type likes social jobs such as teacher, religious worker, counsellor, clinical psychologist, psychiatric case worker, speech therapist. Has social skills and talents, but often lacks mechanical and scientific ability. Is described as:

Convincing	Helpful	Responsible
Cooperative	Idealistic	Sociable
Friendly	Insightful	Tactful
Generous	Kind	Understanding

Enterprising

The Enterprising (E) type likes enterprising jobs such as sales-person, manager, business executive, television producer, sports promoter, buyer. Has leadership and speaking abilities but often lacks scientific ability. Is described as:

Adventurous	Energetic	Self-confident
Ambitious	Impulsive	Sociable
Attention-getting	Optimistic	Popular
Domineering	Pleasure-seeking	

Conventional

The Conventional (C) type likes conventional jobs such as bookkeeper, stenographer, financial analyst, banker, cost estimator, tax expert, Has clerical and arithmetic ability, but often lacks artistic abilities. Is described as:

Conforming	Inhibited	Practical
Conscientious	Obedient	Self-controlled (calm)
Careful	Orderly	Unimaginative
Conservative	Persistent	Efficient

Source: J.L. Holland (1977) *Understanding Yourself and Your Career.* Reproduced by special permission of the publisher, Consulting Psychologists Press, Inc, Palo Alto, California CA 94306.

The resulting summary code reflects the three most significant categories, as far as the client is concerned, for example, IAS. The client then consults the Occupation Finder to see which job titles correspond to the three-letter code. In this case IAS gives Economist, Mathematician/Statician, Market Research Analyst. RIE provides titles such as Watch Repairer, Machine Operator, Furniture Upholsterer, etc. The guide to the Self-Directed Search then discusses the implications of the results for each user, particularly the extent to which they can reliably predict or generate job ideas. Clients are then asked to review their results with family, friends and teachers, and they are invited to seek help from a skilled counsellor.

Holland and others have carried out a good deal of research in support of his six-fold classification system and personality typology mentioned earlier. There seems to be some supporting evidence of the reliability and validity of the Self-Directed Search as a measure of occupational interest. What is likely in future is that research evidence of the usefulness of the Self-Directed Search will come as much from studies of the ways it affects clients' vocational behaviour, their planfulness and self-occupational awareness as from studies of the correlation between the results of the Self-Directed Search and different occupational groups. In other words, its main effectiveness will be in helping students learn about the process of choosing and deciding rather than effecting an accurate match between personalities and type of work.

It is difficult to predict whether interest measures are going to remain a central feature of careers work in this country. The measures of interest and personality described in this chapter are only some of the wide range of tests, interest guides and inventories available to careers practitioners and their clients, and their main aim is to help clients gain a greater awareness of self and obtain insights into their occupational preferences. This increased awareness of self in relation to jobs and work can, of course, be fostered in many different ways and the use of questionnaires, self-rating scales, and self-help materials concerned with the clarification of values, interests and abilities is now widespread. The major problem and difficulty posed by the use of interest measures and questionnaires concerns the process of drawing inferences from the results of such measures to establish the career and occupational areas which a client is likely to find fulfilling. A high score in 'practical and social' interests may all too readily be seen as a clear pointer towards work in nursing or medical careers, when the scores are simply suggesting that the client is, for the moment, expressing some very generalized picture of occupational interests. Indeed, the predictive nature of interest guidance results has always been open to question. This process of drawing inferences from a client's statements of personal preferences to the production of concrete job ideas is precisely the process that computer-based guidance systems attempt to achieve.

The aim of the three most widely used computer-based guidance systems, Cascaid, JIIG-CAL and Gradscope, is to produce job ideas and job titles to match input data concerned with a client's preferences for different kinds of work activity. None of the systems claims to provide a completely accurate assessment of the ideal job for clients; rather, the aim is to generate job ideas with various degree of 'goodness of fit', which will help clients with the career decision-making process. It is then up to individual clients to carry out their own research on the job ideas that have been provided. In terms of the DECIDES mnemonic mentioned earlier, the computer-based careers guidance systems are useful in Identifying alternatives. In discovering probable outcomes, students will have to refer back to occupational information, take part in work experience programmes or speak to employers.

Gradscope

Gradscope, which originated in 1975, was designed specifically for use with students in higher education, but in other ways shares many of the characteristics of Cascaid or JIIG-CAL data systems. Student profiles are matched with a job bank of occupational titles and clients are subsequently provided with a printout of ten occupational suggestions, which they can use as a basis for further information, research or discussion with a counsellor. The student input forms have three separate sections: Work Activities, Abilities and Skills Required and Conditions of Work. Under these three headings students are asked to rate some fifty factors against a five-point rating scale, for example:

Section I Work Activities
    3 Teaching and instruction
   10 Preparing and processing data
Section II Abilities and Skills Required
  21 Being consistently logical
  23 Applying knowledge and skills in new ways
Section III Conditions of Work
  28 Good job security once appointed
  36 Work which is physically demanding

Additional weightings can then be given by clients to those factors which carry special importance or significance. Separate printouts are then provided for client and careers adviser, with a record of the client's responses to the questions posed in the input form.

In evaluating the success of Gradscope, Wilson (1979) refers to a number of field trials that were carried out in six higher education institutions in 1977 and 1978. Two-thirds of the students surveyed thought the system had been of help to them, with three-quarters of them having an interest in three or more of the occupations suggested by the system. No complete research has yet been carried out to see whether there is any correlation between occupations suggested by the system and the kinds of work entered by graduates, and the way students use the results in information search and counselling interviews has yet to be clearly established. The system is, however, widely used by university careers services. It is estimated that it may be coping on a national basis with 10,000 inputs per year.

More recently an interactive version of Gradscope has been developed for use with microcomputers which provides occupational information, immediate printout facility and allows students to change their answers and undertake a number of sub-routines. Evaluatory studies of the interactive version suggest that students often benefit considerably by using it on a self-help and unsupervised basis, often spending three-quarters of an hour running through the program before consulting a careers adviser. As with other interactive programs, there seems to be a far greater possibility of enabling the client's careers decision-making process than is the case with programs which are supported by centrally administered batch processing services.

Cascaid

The Cascaid system was developed by the Leicestershire Careers Service initially for use by students at secondary school level. A separate version also exists for students in higher education. The aim is to produce a list of career suggestions relevant to the 'occupational activity preferences' of each client. In the Cascaid-HE version, for example, students are asked to consider fifty-three statements about functions and relationships in the work environment and assess each of these against a five-point rating scale (see Figure 4.5). Students are then asked to consider key preferences, give details of any physical illnesses or disabilities and give an indication of any careers they are actively considering. As with Gradscope and JIIG-CAL, the resulting profile is then matched with, in this particular case, some 200 career titles. The final printout then evaluates the careers being actively considered by the student in terms of the goodness of fit with the way the client has answered the input questions, provides a list of jobs that are good matches with the client's responses and, finally, provides details of 'fair' matches, that is, jobs and careers which may be worth consideration by the client, although they may not represent strongly liked activities.

In their statement of rationale for the system, the staff of the Cascaid Unit have taken pains to point out that a high degree of

Figure 4.5. Entry Form for CASCAID Higher Education

* Before starting read through all the statements * Remember that each statement should be prefaced by "HOW WOULD YOU LIKE A JOB WHICH REQUIRES YOU TO ...."	LIKE VERY MUCH	LIKE	NEUTRAL	DISLIKE	DIS-LIKE VERY MUCH	
07	Use an aptitude for mathematical techniques	1	2	3	4	5	39
08	Use arithmetical and basic statistical skills	1	2	3	4	5	
09	Address or talk to groups of people	1	2	3	4	5	
10	Gather information	1	2	3	4	5	
11	Write up formal reports	1	2	3	4	5	
12	Use a foreign language — after training if necessary	1	2	3	4	5	B1
14	Communicate extensively through the written word	1	2	3	4	5	
15	Undertake systematic analysis of information	1	2	3	4	5	
19	Employ a sensitivity for design, colour and shape	1	2	3	4	5	
20	Be subjected to an element of personal physical risk	1	2	3	4	5	
23	Have to work outside regularly irrespective of weather conditions	1	2	3	4	5	
26	Use technical equipment after appropriate training	1	2	3	4	5	
27	Prepare diagrammatic display of information	1	2	3	4	5	
31	Interpret diagrammatic display of information	1	2	3	4	5	
33	Use physical effort	1	2	3	4	5	B2
35	Care for and give treatment to people who are physically ill	1	2	3	4	5	
36	Care for and give treatment to people who are mentally ill	1	2	3	4	5	
37	Care for and give treatment to people who are physically handicapped	1	2	3	4	5	
38	Care for and give treatment to people who are mentally sub-normal	1	2	3	4	5	
41	Be persuasive	1	2	3	4	5	
42	Help others to solve their personal or social problems	1	2	3	4	5	
43	Become actively involved in providing facilities for a local community	1	2	3	4	5	
44	Be involved with the Arts but not as a performer	1	2	3	4	5	B3
45	Train and educate others	1	2	3	4	5	

46	Be involved with education but not as a teacher	1	2	3	4	5	
48	Observe and evaluate the behaviour of others, THEN act on your conclusions	1	2	3	4	5	
50	Make recommendations based on your professional expertise	1	2	3	4	5	B3
52	Cope with members of the public face to face	1	2	3	4	5	
55	Deal with representatives of other organisations	1	2	3	4	5	
56	Have considerable working contact with other departments within your own organisation	1	2	3	4	5	
57	Work towards solutions through negotiation and haggling	1	2	3	4	5	
60	Have contact with children up to the age of 11	1	2	3	4	5	
61	Have contract with young people aged 11 to 18	1	2	3	4	5	
67	Organise leisure and recreation facilities	1	2	3	4	5	
69	Maintain and improve the quality of the environment	1	2	3	4	5	B4
71	Use an interest in history	1	2	3	4	5	
75	Interpret legislation and regulations	1	2	3	4	5	
76	Enforce legislation and regulations	1	2	3	4	5	
78	Deal with financial matters	1	2	3	4	5	
79	Assess the monetary value of goods and services	1	2	3	4	5	
80	Directly supervise the activities of other workers	1	2	3	4	5	
81	Organise and administer the work of others	1	2	3	4	5	
83	Actively investigate complex systems and procedures	1	2	3	4	5	
84	Adhere to clearly defined procedures and use your judgement and initiative within those limits	1	2	3	4	5	
86	Deal with documentation	1	2	3	4	5	B5
87	Be involved with freight and passenger transportation	1	2	3	4	5	
91	Study for a formal professional qualification as part of your work	1	2	3	4	5	
92	Serve in the Navy/WRNS	1	2	3	4	5	
93	Serve in the Army/WRAC	1	2	3	4	5	
94	Serve in the RAF/WRAF	1	2	3	4	5	
95	Have a fixed base but work regularly at other locations within easy daily travelling distance	1	2	3	4	5	89
97	Be absent from home regularly	1	2	3	4	5	
99	Work regularly outside the normal 9–5 pattern	1	2	3	4	5	

consistency and credibility is required in producing occupational suggestions. In purposely omitting extrinsic job factors from the system, for
example, salary, social prestige, they have sought to concentrate solely
on intrinsic job functions, while recognizing that:

> individual jobs in any occupational group will vary according to the
> importance of specific functions;
> not every job function will be a source of satisfaction to individuals
> performing that particular job;
> the occupational suggestions will be acceptable to the client only if
> there is a close identification with the primary or core functions in
> any particular job and at least a tolerance of the majority of less
> central functions as defined by the program.

The authors' claim that careers suggestions should provide a
realistic basis for discussion between counsellor and client may stimulate a client's self-assessment and information searches and generally
may widen the horizons of those whose career knowledge is restricted to
occupational stereotypes.

Cascaid was originally designed to be used in a batch mode —
completed questionnaires were sent for processing at a central location
and then returned with a printout of the results. The career titles are
ranked with the title having the most appropriate working heading.
Each title is then printed with the profile of the student's responses.
Microcomputer interactive versions of Cascaid now exist which allow
students to vary their responses, reflect on the input they have made
and then question the program as to why certain occupational titles have
not appeared in their suggested list. Occupational suggestions then
appear on a monitor rather than in print form.

The advantages of the Cascaid system are that it provides a useful
framework for discussion between counsellor and student. It is in part a
process which encourages self-awareness in relation to jobs. In the
microcomputer system, in particular, it allows students to take an active
role in their career planning and decision-making and they can if they
wish use the system without reference to a careers adviser. Like most of
the British systems, however, it operates on a simple matching of clients
and occupational suggestions which is based on the client's preferences
concerning intrinsic job features and activities. In reality, however,
occupational choice may be dependent to an equal degree on other
factors, such as clients' occupational stereotypes; perceived occupational
status; the likelihood of personal success; peer group influence; or the
orientation of personal values.

JIIG-CAL

JIIG-CAL (Job Ideas and Information Generator/Computer Assisted Learning) developed by Closs and Broderick is an extension of the APU Occupational Interests Guide described earlier. The aim of the system is to provide careers advisers and clients with job ideas and to supply information about each job and its entry requirements. Like Cascaid and Gradscope, the system operates with clients listing anticipated qualifications, health factors and the results of the APU interest guide which are then matched with job titles in the computer job file. Like other computer-based guidance systems, its aim is clearly to aid the client's decision-making, and even to carry out the decision-making on the client's behalf, by synthesizing information about the client's interests, abilities, likes and dislikes, with the demands of different occupational areas.

Perhaps the most interesting feature of the JIIG-CAL system is that its rationale is clearly concerned with careers education, and it seems Closs has acknowledged an important shift of emphasis in careers work from that of diagnostic guidance to education and counselling. It has been expressly designed for classroom use and Figure 4.6 indicates how the administration and preparation for JIIG-CAL can be programmed for use in schools. In describing its use as an educational tool, Closs (1980) suggests that

> The JIIG-CAL system is an educational tool for use under normal classroom conditions. It is designed to fit easily into an ongoing careers education programme. Beginning in the second last year of normal schooling (Scottish S3, English 4th year) pupils first learn how to use the system by themselves. From then until they leave school they may use it as frequently as they wish or as the school will permit.

Closs goes further by suggesting that a major aim of the system is that of stimulating self-assessment and encouraging students to match themselves against the occupational suggestions. This clearly stated careers education rationale is surprising, given the previous history of the APU guide and its use in diagnostic vocational guidance settings — it amounts to a very distinct shift in emphasis towards greater pupil and client autonomy in effecting career decisions.

The output from the JIIG-CAL system also distinguishes it from the other computer-based systems in that it not only presents lists of job titles with a points rating indicating the level of suitability, but also brief job descriptions (with normal and maxi printouts), special entry require-

Figure 4.6.   The Use of JIIG-CAL in Classroom Settings

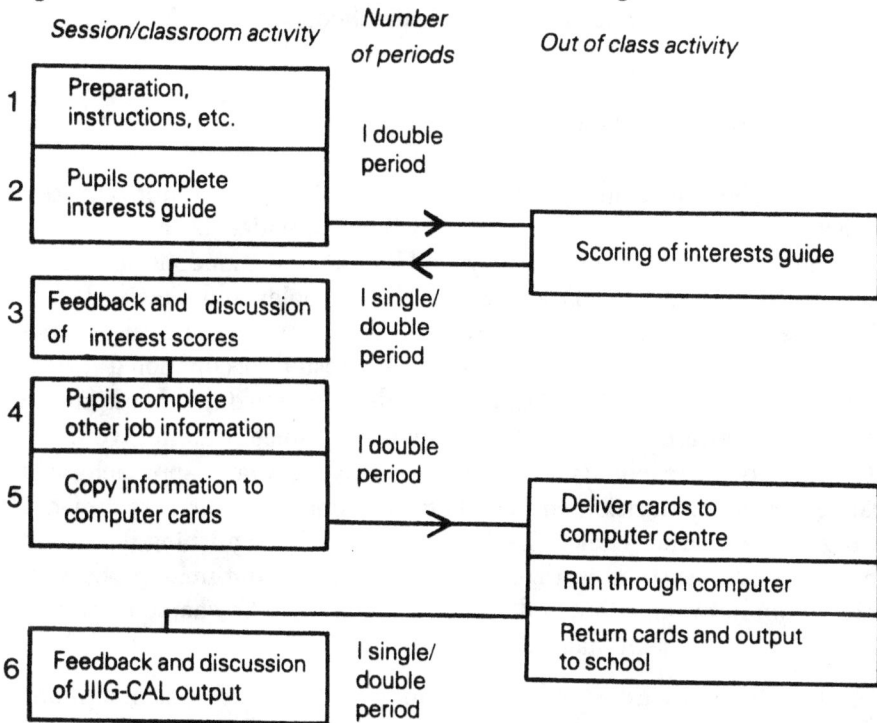

Source: S.J. Closs (1983) *JIIG-CAL Information Booklet,* Release III. Reproduced by permission of the anthor.

ments and training profiles, together with suggestions for further reading and pointers to other sources of occupational information.

Another distinguishing feature of the JIIG-CAL system is the different levels of usage. At a basic level, the interests profile can be employed on its own, scored individually, and used as a basis for individual counselling. At a second level, the interests guide can be used independently of the remainder of the system and is based on computer scoring. Alternatively the full JIIG-CAL system can be used which consists of two separate stages or procedures — one concerned with the interests guide and one concerned with the matching of client information with job suggestions. At a further level still, JIIG-CAL can be used with the computer assisted learning system in the design of careers education programmes.

Evaluation studies of the JIIG-CAL system show that it is effective in increasing occupational awareness and providing students with job ideas. Students, it seems, find it easy to complete and record largely positive responses to its use. How far it is able to encourage self-awareness has, it seems, yet to be researched.

MAUD and SELSTRA

Arguably the most interesting development in computer assisted careers counselling in this country has been provided by two systems designed by the Decision Analysis Unit at the London School of Economics, called MAUD and SELSTRA (Wooler and Lewis, 1982). Whereas the systems described earlier operate by scanning an occupational data base to provide a list of suggested occupational titles, MAUD's central aim is to aid the careers decision-making process and to raise clients' awareness of the determinants of choice. In other words, it attempts to make clients aware of the way they are approaching a particular career decision and elicits from them the constructs they are using in their career choice (Kelly, 1955). The distinguishing feature of this particular system is that it operates by a continual process of interaction between client and computer which can be characterized by a number of different stages.

1   Clients are asked to list the number of career or decision options they are presently considering. MAUD then evaluates, by questioning, the factor that the client is using to distinguish between the options under consideration. It could be, for example, that 'immediate entry without further training' is the major construct clients are using to assess their career options, other factors could include 'pay' or 'long-term prospects'.
2   Having established all the significant factors affecting career choice, MAUD evaluates each career option, for example, banking or social work against each of the elicited factors.
3   MAUD then sets out to determine how important, relatively, the client believes each factor to be. (For example, a 'personally rewarding' job may be more important than 'pay'.)
4   Finally, MAUD aggregates all the information provided by the client concerning options and decision factors to provide a preference order and score for each career options.

It should be stressed that clients are free at all times to change their minds and amend their input to the computer and, if the final preference order is at odds with the client's own intuitive feelings of preference, more information about decision factors may by added to provide a complete picture of all the variables at work in the client's career choice.

SELSTRA is another interactive program designed initially for use by students in higher education. Rather than elicit from clients a list of factors that are being used in a decision-making process, SELSTRA presents the client with a 'core' or hierarchy of factors which research has suggested are significant to students about to graduate. The 'core' of factors can be broken down into three distinct groups:

those which make the job intrinsically interesting;
those concerned with the availability of job opportunities; and
those which concern the way a particular job fits in with non-work
life.

Clients are then asked to give some further elaboration to the three sets of factors and generate other statement/factors which form an individualized tree (see Figure 4.7). Career or job options are then scored against the factors in the hierarchical tree.

Figure 4.7.   *Hierarchy of 'Core' Factors Built into Current Version of SELSTRA*

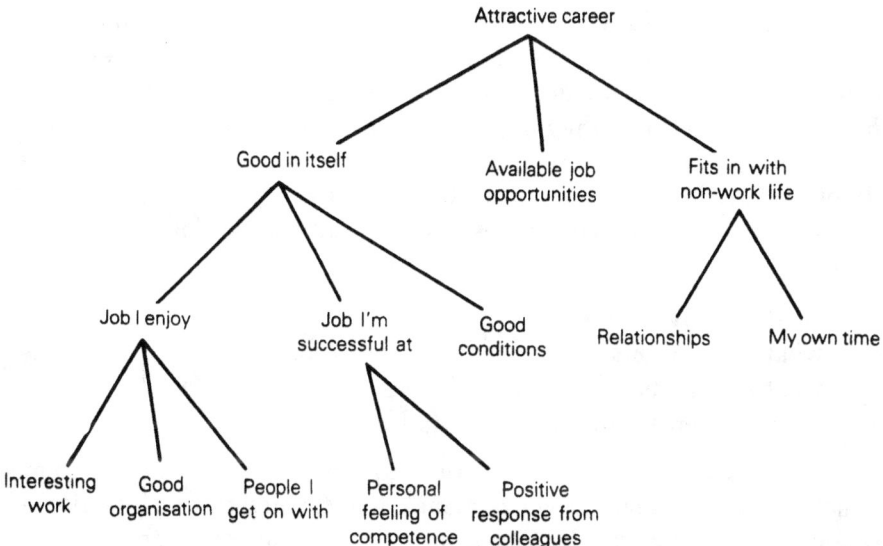

Source: S. Wooler and B. Lewis (1982) 'Computer Assisted Careers Counselling: A New Approach', *British Journal of Guidance and Counselling*, 10, pp. 124–34. Reproduced by permission of Hobsons Press (Cambridge) Ltd., publishers of·all CRAC materials.

Like MAUD, SELSTRA is an entirely interactive program and can be used by clients without reference to a counsellor. However, a major aim of those who have developed both programs is that the counsellor's experience can be added to the insights gained from the use of the program to provide a satisfactory outcome to the helping interview; for maximum effectiveness it is, therefore, necessary for the careers counsellor to work through the program with the client in a step by step process. MAUD and SELSTRA are not intended for use on a 'stand alone' basis, but within the context of a careers counselling interview. Both programs require the careers counsellor to act as intermediary in elaborating the factors which the client is employing in the career decision-making process.

While many of the examples of British computer-based careers guidance systems are in an early stage of development, American systems have existed for sometime. Two interactive systems, based on decision learning, SIGI (System of Interactive Guidance and Information) and DISCOVER, were developed in the early seventies and have both been widely used and tested.

SIGI, developed by Martin Katz, is an interactive system designed to help college students make rational and informed career decisions. It uses a multiple choice format to student responses in six major stages or subsystems: Values, Locate, Compare, Prediction, Planning and Strategy. Users first clarify their values, specify value statements, compare different occupations, predict their chances of success in given fields and plan how they can enter the occupations in the SIGI databank. The emphasis in the SIGI system is not on providing the 'right' choice, but on helping the student in the process of choosing, as part of that choice process helps students answer the following questions:

> what are my values?
> what occupations correspond with my value statements?
> what chance have I of entering particular occupations?
> how do I enter one particular field?

Like SIGI, DISCOVER is also a comprehensive interactive system, which helps users survey their personal values, study the organization of occupations and assess interests; it provides information on training and occupational entry in twenty-one separate modules. John Holland's 'Self Directed Search' is included in the system. Users may select any entry point, but if they choose to work through the entire system, it would take some ten to twelve hours to complete. Evaluative studies of both SIGI and DISCOVER have been carried out extensively. In one study of the use of SIGI, 70 per cent of users said they would recommend the system to their friends and over 60 per cent wanted to use the system again in the future.

So what implications are there for the use of careers guidance systems in Britain and the use of computers in the careers counselling process? Two trends in particular are discernible. Firstly, it is clear that clients will have far easier access to occupational information than ever before. The DOORS system (Data on Occupations: Retrieval System), developed by Manpower Services Commission, will be available in 1984 in all MSC Job Libraries, giving occupational information, data on entry qualifications, earnings and hours of work for 800–1000 different occupations. A national database of occupational information will therefore be available to the public. There are, of course, systems already in use in local authority careers services for vacancy matching and maintaining records of local employers on employer databases (Collins, 1982). Developments of this kind will eventually enable careers practitioners to relinquish many of the information-giving aspects of their work and expand other areas.

Secondly, it seems certain that there will be an increased use of interactive microcomputer programs as part of the careers counselling process. MAUD and SELSTRA represent the beginning of an exciting period of development of interactive careers guidance programmes and systems which will help clients with the self-awareness and decision learning process which form the major part of most careers counselling interviews. One major development in the next five years is likely to be that of a fully integrated British system for all students in higher education. The Computer Aided Careers Guidance System (C-ACGS) will, like the American interactive systems, help users to learn to make career decisions, by facilitating exploration of the self and the world of work, and help students formulate personal career objectives and plan a course of action. Despite the comprehensiveness and apparent complexity of new interactive systems, however, it seems likely that many of these microcomputer systems will not operate on a 'standalone' basis and that careers practitioners will work alongside their clients in working through the processes of choice, decision-making and self assessment.

Chapter 5

Helping Agencies and Transition Services

In this country, careers guidance is largely an educational enterprise, carried out by careers teachers in schools, careers officers employed by local education authorities and institution-based careers advisers in institutions of further and higher education. A cursory view of the history and the development of what Reubens (1977) calls transition agencies in this country shows, however, that both state employment and education agencies have had competing claims on youth employment services in particular. Successive legislation embodied in the Employment and Training Acts of 1948 and 1973 has ensured that the provision of a careers service is a mandatory obligation for local education authorities rather than a centralized function of manpower and employment agencies. The 1973 Employment and Training Act also removed the previous age limit of 18, enabling the Careers Service to provide a service for clients of all ages leaving educational centres, and indeed there is nothing to prevent LEAs from providing guidance and placement services for adults as well as those under 18. In practice, however, few have chosen to do so with any degree of commitment. In the main, the focus for careers guidance and counselling activity has been on clients leaving educational institutions, whether statutory age school leavers or graduates leaving universities and polytechnics. As a result, the agencies themselves — the Careers Services, university and polytechnic careers and appointments services — have taken on the role of bridging agencies between the worlds of education and employment.

Slightly different models of careers counselling intervention exist in Europe and the United States. In France *conseillers d'orientation* appointed by the Ministry of Education provide careers guidance to school leavers and students in higher education at university guidance units (Cellules d'Information et d'Orientation, CIO) which are managed and financed by the universities themselves. In West Germany all careers guidance is provided by a national, centralized Federal Employment Institute dealing with clients aged 16 upwards, in which *Berufs-berater* (careers counsellors) are seen as distinct from placement officers or *Arbeitsberater*. In Sweden both education and manpower agencies cooperate to provide an educationally-based career guidance service in which consultants, similar to careers officers, financed by local education authorities visit a number of schools to interview students. As in the UK separate facilities and services exist for university students. In contrast to European countries, the United States has no national, centralized transition agency or indeed policy for guidance services. Instead, individual schools and colleges act as the focal point for cooperation with employers, the employment service and the community, and provide career education and counselling for their own students. Individual states have their own careers guidance policies and practices. As Reubens points out in her comprehensive review of international transition agencies, each developed country has a different policy and accords varying degrees of funding to the helping agencies concerned with careers counselling, but, with the exception of the United States, most of the Western countries and Japan have developed centrally administered guidance and transition agencies for young people in particular. And despite slight differences in administration and organization, the transition services have broadly similar sets of objectives in the provision of occupational information, individual counselling and orientation and careers programmes concerned with work ethics and values, social and personal competencies, occupational implications of educational choices, job characteristics and requirements, occupational outlook, psycho-social aspects of the work role and social and economic institutions. In concluding her comparative analysis, Reubens (1977) identifies seven features which characterize careers counselling and guidance provision in advanced countries:

1 establishment of the full range of transition services as a comprehensive, integrated whole;
2 a national commitment to provide the transition services throughout the country, reinforced by legislation which defines the responsibilities of the various levels and branches of government;
3 creation of special organizational structures and personnel to deal with the difficult operation of spanning two worlds;
4 sharing of responsibilities between the educational and the labour market authorities, between the schools and the employment service;
5 acceptance of the transition function by the schools;

6 frequent adaptation and improvement of programmes in response to changes in the educational system, patterns of
attendance, youth life styles, and the youth labour market;

7 genuine participation in policy, planning, and operations by
employers and their organizations, trade unions, community
organizations, and other concerned groups.

The aim of the remainder of this chapter is to describe the range of
careers guidance and transition agencies which exists in this country and
to point to the way they operate in practice. In the main it will be seen
that careers counselling and guidance is the responsibility of education
services and that job placement is that of the state employment
agencies.

The Work of the Careers Service

The principal careers counselling services in the UK are provided by
local education authorities under the 1973 Employment and Training
Act. The Careers Service has the role of transition agency — its aim is to
help individuals leaving full-time education to make a satisfactory
transition to school or college from work. In its outlook, the Careers
Service is also a bridging agency, providing a link between the worlds of
education and of industry and commerce. The three principal objectives
of LEA Careers Services as defined by the Department of Employment's memorandum of guidance are as follows:

> ... to seek to ensure that the pupils, students and staff of
> schools and colleges are fully aware of the demands that working
> life is likely to make on young people entering employment, and
> on the scope and range of opportunities available to them;
>
> to provide, in association with schools and colleges, vocational
> guidance to pupils and students in schools and colleges at
> appropriate stages during their educational life;
>
> to help young people leaving schools and colleges and those who
> are unemployed, to find employment, education or training, or
> places on appropriate special schemes.

It is important to mention at this stage that although each LEA is
responsible for running its own careers service, the Secretary of State for
Employment gives general guidance to authorities in England on the
conduct of their careers services and oversees their operation on behalf
of central government. Similar responsibilities are exercised in respect

of the services in Scotland and Wales by the appropriate Secretaries of State. This dual control over management of LEA careers services is the legacy of the conflicting claims on the part of the Education and Labour Ministries in the early part of this century ever since the Juvenile Employment Service was first established.

The range of objectives given to the Careers Services has left it with a multiplicity of different functions concerned with individual clients, developing careers work in schools and liaising with employing organizations (see Figure 5.1). Having ascribed to itself the role of bridging agency, the Careers Service has found itself with a wide range of tasks and activities, which it seems has often led to a poorly defined conception of its role.

Figure 5.1. Careers Service Functions

Concerned with face to face work with clients	• careers interviews • provision of occupational information • talks/careers lectures/group discussions • review of progress for those already in work • placement for YTS or work • organizing events, e.g. careers conventions • monitoring those on unemployment register
Connected with schools and teachers	• instigation of in-service training events for teachers • planning and contributions to school-based careers programmes • providing and distributing careers information
Connected with employers and training agencies	• canvassing job vacancies • helping with pre-selection • occupational visits and job studies • visiting YTS schemes • assembling data on local employment markets

Staffing and Work-Load

Local education authority Careers Services have increased steadily in staff size since the Employment and Training Act, with 5080 Careers Officers, employment assistants and other support staff in England alone. With the rise in youth unemployment the government has funded directly a number of posts (850 in England) specifically to help the young unemployed, and this additional support from central government, circumventing the rate support grant settlements, is likely to continue.

The organizational structure of Careers Services in LEAs is broadly the same throughout the country, with senior posts of responsibility going to those Careers Officers who administer staff over a geographical area and those who take posts of special responsibility. While each authority has to comply with the essential features of the Act, each sets its own policy. In practice there can be quite significant differences in the assumptions of different Principal Careers Officers about the kind of provision they offer and priorities given to various aspects of their work. Specialist Careers Officer posts exist for work with the unemployed and disabled. 'Handicapped Specialists' will visit special schools and interview pupils, much as ordinary Careers Officers would, although their work will take on the character of individual case-work requiring continual contact with other referral agencies, such as the Disablement Rehabilitation Service, and with specialist training centres and training workshops where accurate assessments can be made of young people's skill levels.

Specialist posts also exist for work with the academically more able, and Careers Officers are expected to become familiar with entry and qualification details in the higher education system and with professional training. They will also be expected to keep informed about trends in graduate employment. In some authorities, specialist posts also exist for staff involved in industrial liaison and careers information work. The number and variety of these posts of special responsibility in the Careers Service in part reflect the wide variety of functions undertaken, but also the need to provide some measure of career development for staff in the service, for, generally speaking, all specialist posts enjoy higher salary gradings.

Work with Clients

The main feature of a Careers Officer's work is one-to-one interviewing with students in schools and colleges. Interview programmes may begin in the fourth year, but the bulk of a Careers Officer's interviews will take place in years 5 and 6 of secondary schooling with students on courses of general education. Careers Officers based in colleges of further education may also see a large number of students on vocational courses at the post-16 stage. The number of interviews with school pupils rose from

573,000 in 1974 to 744,000 in 1981. Greater percentage increases occurred in the number of interviews with college students (rising from 32,500 to 80,000) in the same period.

The exact aim and nature of a Careers Officer's school-based interviews is open to question and it may be that the client's perception is none too clear, leading to unrealistic expectations of the interview outcomes — a common problem for all careers practitioners. For some Careers Officers first interviews may be genuine attempts at vocational counselling; on other occasions interviews will be more a matter of screening young people's career intentions, generally helping with their career plans or providing information on training courses or employment opportunities. Whatever the exact nature of school-based careers interviews, it is clear that they do not correspond to the vocational or diagnostic guidance interview mentioned in the Employment and Training Act and there would seem to be a considerable degree of mismatch between official expectations of the result of individual interviews and what takes place in practice. This lack of agreement about what can realistically be achieved in half-hour interviews is reflected in the debate which has raged at least fifteen years in the Careers Service about whether Careers Officers should 'blanket' interview every school leaver or concentrate on those students who elect to see them. This debate is itself symptomatic of the lack of a clear conceptualization of the purpose of a careers interview — an issue which was referred to in an earlier chapter.

Naturally, interviews taking place in careers offices, especially when concerned with immediate placement, may take on a different set of characteristics from the more exploratory kind undertaken in schools. In carrying out their school-based interviews, Careers Officers have access to school reports, often results of interest questionnaires and, more recently, print-outs from computer-based guidance systems. At the time of writing sixty-seven local education authorities subscribe to Cascaid (see Chapter 4).

Careers officers also see students in groups in schools and colleges as part of careers education programmes, principally to describe the role of the Careers Service and to acquaint students with the administrative procedures concerning school leaving and work and YTS entry. While school-based work has not increased in the period 1974–81, the amount of work with students in colleges of further education has almost doubled. This suggests that as students stay in the education system for longer periods past the statutory school leaving age Careers Officers will delay their involvement in careers programmes. Certainly, there is considerable evidence to suggest that, with increasing youth unemployment and the introduction of the Youth Training Scheme, Careers Officers will gradually withdraw from much school-based work.

Two further features of the Careers Service's role with clients need to be mentioned. Firstly, the Careers Service has an important role in disseminating careers information to schools in LEAs and developing their own careers information resource centres, which are available to clients who use the Careers Office. Secondly, while the Careers Service ceased the payment of unemployment and supplementary benefit as a result of the 1973 Act, Careers Service staff are still required to inform the Department of Health and Social Security if young people become ineligible for benefit to ensure that unemployed young people do continue to register at Careers Offices. To an outside observer, this monitoring role with the unemployed may well seem to mitigate against any positive initiatives with unemployed groups and to inhibit Careers Officers taking a fully client-centred role.

Careers Officers' Involvement in Schools

As already mentioned, a large proportion of a Careers Officer's time is spent in school-based careers interviews with fourth, fifth or sixth year pupils. They also contribute actively to other parts of schools' careers programmes, by carrying out group discussion sessions, arranging careers conventions and attending parents' evenings. Considerable cooperation is required between Careers Officer and careers teacher if school-based careers programmes are to achieve any measure of success. The careers service has also seen itself playing an active role in fostering the development of school-based work. It is only in the last twenty years that careers teachers have begun to be appointed and that careers education has gained recognition as a valid curricular component. Throughout this period LEA Careers Services have taken on a training and development role by providing short courses and general support for careers teachers. In some areas, for example, the Principal Careers Officer has a specific responsibility for advising the local education authority on careers education in schools and on the appointment of careers teachers, and often the Careers Service has been responsible for developing local careers associations for careers teachers and Careers Officers alike. It seems likely, however, that with continuing pressure of resources and the problems presented by youth unemployment, Careers Officers will, in future, spend less time in schools, particularly on one-to-one interviewing. It will be interesting to see whether the gradual withdrawal of Careers Officers from schools will see an increased activity on the part of careers teachers, with a commensurate increase in their time allowance for careers education.

Work in Placement and Employment

Careers Services have sought to maintain close links with local employers, both for their own professional practice — carrying out job studies and increasing their own stock of information about employment opportunities — and to provide vacancies for their clients. Since the dramatic rise in youth unemployment, Careers Services have made special efforts to canvass employers for vacancies and have undertaken publicity schemes involving local media and employer groups. In 1977 Careers Officers in England carried out 45,000 visits to improve their labour market knowledge. In 1981 this figure had increased to 77,000. Routine meetings with employers and employer visits for the purposes of job study have shown similar increases.

Despite this increased activity connected with employer liaison, the number of young people placed in work by the Careers Service continues to decline, presumably because the vacancies simply do not exist in any numbers. As Figure 5.2 shows, placings in YOP far exceeded those in employment and it seems likely that this trend will continue with the introduction in 1983 of the New Training Scheme. One positive result of the increased attention to local labour markets is that many Careers Services have been able to improve the occupational information provided to their clients and many now produce handbooks indicating the major employment areas and training opportunities.

Undoubtedly the single most important influence on the recent work of the Careers Service has been the dramatic rise in youth unemployment and central government's range of measures to provide training and work experience for the young unemployed school leaver. In 1981 approximately one in two statutory age school leavers took part in YOP schemes of one kind or another, 550,000 places in all. In 1982/83, estimates suggest that the Youth Opportunities Programme had provided 100,000 new training places and almost all of the placement of young people into YOP schemes was carried out by local authority Careers Services. As a consequence, careers services placings into YOP far outnumbered those in employment. The size and scope of central government's (MSC) financing of Careers Service personnel has already been mentioned and it is clear that this direct investment by a central government agency in what is fundamentally a local education authority enterprise has meant a change in the way local authority

Figure 5.2. *Placings by Careers Service into Youth Opportunity Programmes (YOP) and Employment*

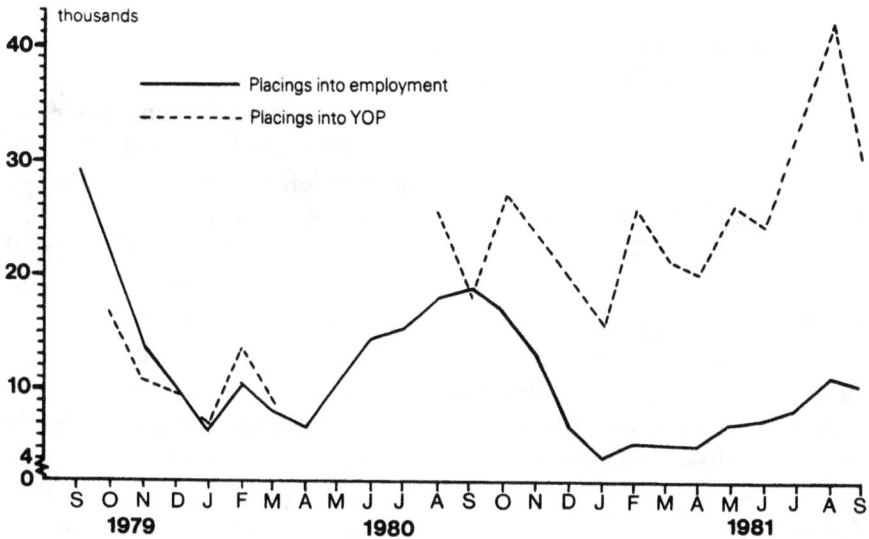

Notes and Sources: All figures relate to placements by the Careers Service in England. Placings into employment are derived from Careers Service Return EDS 81/81A. Placings into YOP are derived from MSC Special Programmes Division Return SP16A. Figures for the period April–July 1980 were not available from Special Programmes Division.

Careers Services operate and in the work of individual Careers Officers.

For Careers Officers have not just been responsible for placement into YOP schemes but also for placement of those who have completed their YOP work experience or training. Furthermore, one of the characteristics of YOP schemes was their local or regional delivery supervised by Special Programmes Area Boards, and it is clear that Careers Service staff have been involved in the planning of the provision for YOP schemes in their local areas. In addition, it is envisaged that as part of the Youth Training Scheme Careers Officers will be actively involved in providing guidance for young people while they are engaged in a training placement. As Knasel *et al.* (1982) point out, this activity could well bring Careers Officers similar role confusion and conflict as it has done previously with careers teachers, in that YTS trainers themselves will see it as their role to provide overall support and guidance for their trainees. It will certainly demand greater interagency collaboration if a successful support and guidance system for trainees is to be established.

Youth unemployment has also had an influence on the way local authority Careers Services operate. At least one authority has abandoned its idea of a centrally administered careers office in favour of a programme of basing Careers Officers in schools to form 'pastoral bases' for those about to leave and those who have left school, so that Careers Officers can be in close contact with their client groups.

Other services are carrying out an increasing amount of work with the young unemployed by appointing 'outreach' officers to visit youth centres, again in order to stay in contact with their clients.

It seems likely that the work of Careers Officers will undergo a period of regular if not dramatic change in the foreseeable future, largely because of structural changes in the economy and because of the impact of these changes on the life chances of those now leaving the educational system. Instead of placing young people into work, many Careers Officers will now be placing them in training schemes, or helping their clients through the maze of post-16 education and training provision. This complexity of provision of courses and qualifications for 16–19-year-olds is well documented by Locke and Bloomfield (1982). With increasing numbers of students remaining for longer periods in both secondary and further education, it would seem as though Careers Officers would be centrally placed to help students make sense of the further education and training system and map their way through the various qualification routes. Counselling students about education and training routes may, therefore, play a larger part in the Careers Officer's role than counselling concerned with work entry and job placement.

It remains to be seen whether this will make the Careers Service less of a bridging agency between school and work or whether, as seems unlikely, Careers Officers will need to do less placement work, have less contact with employers, but spend more time counselling the young unemployed about further education, training and work experience. What seems clear is that Careers Services will have to determine some order of priorities in the wide range of functions undertaken by them. There seems to be no clear consensus on what these priorities may be and in what direction changes may occur. At the same time as Ashton and McGuire (1980) urge the Careers Service to improve the quality of its knowledge of local labour markets and thus enhance its professional autonomy and placement role, Devine (1981) argues that Careers Officers should develop further their roles as professional counsellors and imbue their work with greater client-centredness. Clearly, at a time of diminishing resources it is difficult to develop in a number of different directions at the same time. As one Principal Careers Officer (Loudon, 1982) indicates, there is still considerable ambiguity and confusion concerning the role of the Careers Service:

> Much time continues to be expended in discussing the complementary conflicting roles of careers teacher and careers officer in territorial battles with other youth organisations, and its status claims based on the number of young unemployed and the special relationship which the Careers Service would have with them, were the additional resources available.

The Evaluation of the Work of the Careers Service

The confusion about the exact role of the Careers Service is reflected in attempts that have been made to measure its success as a transition agency and evaluate its work with clients. As one would expect, the Department of Employment's Careers Service Branch is interested mainly in a quantitative analysis of the work of the service and collects information on the number of guidance interviews and group sessions carried out annually. The evidence (Department of Employment, 1982) shows a pattern of continuing increase in Careers Service activity in the last eight years.

Evidence to show the usefulness of the service to clients has been more difficult to obtain. Clarke (1980c) comments that surveys of young people's perceptions of the influence and helpfulness of the Careers Service have generally yielded unsatisfactory if not uncomplimentary results. By and large this is because researchers have used inappropriate methodology in assessing the work of the service, and in a number of transition studies have asked questions, about the perceived helpfulness of the service, of clients who may have had little access to or use of the services in the first place.

In reviewing the work of Douglas (1971) and Thomas and Wetherall (1974), Clarke (1980b) concludes: 'Research findings suggest that the perceived influence of the Careers Service tends to be slight and is far less potent than advice from informal sources.' The words 'influence' and 'advice' are significant here for they assume a directive and placement role to which the Careers Service cannot really lay claim, and at the same time fail to acknowledge the generally facilitative and helpful role most Careers Officers would adopt.

Maizels (1970), Roberts (1971) and Willis (1977) all lament the fact that the Careers Service is not more influential in increasing a student's life chances and in determining the kinds of work entered by young people, when in truth most Careers Officers accepting a developmental model for their work would probably welcome the fact that parents are the major influence on a young person's choice of job or that young people can decide for themselves, rather than accept a Careers Officer's recommendation. Other studies have been content to examine the placement function alone, rather than acknowledge the wide range of functions undertaken by the Careers Service.

More recently, research has been carried out on the developmental stage reached by the experimental subject group and on the usefulness of Careers Officer interviews. Bedford (1982a) providing a preliminary report of an extensive study of Careers Officer interviews, claims that they are a strong stimulus to the career planning of fifth year students in school. Further research of this kind, which takes into account a developmental rationale for occupational choice and monitors the total effectiveness of the Careers Service in facilitating students' career thinking, will be beneficial to both Careers Officers and clients.

The Role of Schools in Careers Counselling and Guidance

Careers work in school is still poorly developed and the Department of Education and Science Survey 18 concluded, for example, that 'effective careers education is often handicapped by services' lack of time by both teachers and pupils.' These twin themes of lack of manpower and lack of time occur with regular frequency when school-based careers education and guidance services are under review.

Much therefore depends on the personal commitment of head-teachers to the idea of school-based careers work, and this accounts for the wide variety of provision and practice. Some schools, for example, have well stocked careers information and seminar rooms, a Head of Careers appointed at a senior level who has an adequate time allowance for careers teaching, interviewing and administration. Other schools have no provision at all. There is no guarantee that a particular student will have access to a careers programme in school, or be able to explore his or her career aspirations in a helping interview. This is particularly true of more able pupils, particularly those in selective schools.

This lack of commitment on the part of some schools extends, of course, to careers education, which like other curriculum components concerned with personal rather than academic development, for example, social and health education, finds itself competing for a share of curriculum time in the face of calls for higher standards and emphasis on academic subjects. A common situation faced by careers teachers in schools is one in which a meagre time allowance is made for careers work, coupled with a reluctance to give careers education any curriculum time.

Some progress has been made. As DES Survey 18, 'Careers Education in Secondary Schools', points out, the 1960s saw a general acknowledgment of the importance of the school to work transition and the role of the careers teacher. It was in 1969, for example, that the National Association of Careers Teachers (now NACGT) was formed to encourage the development of good career guidance practice in schools. Since then considerable developments have been made in the provision of published careers education materials and resources and in the quality of what is carried out by careers teachers and coordinators, even if there has been no commensurate increase in the time allowance and manpower resources devoted to the particular subject. It is interesting to compare, for example, the results of DES survey 18 with the more recent HMI report, *Aspects of Secondary Education* (1979). The earlier report documents that 94 per cent of schools in England and Wales designate at least one member of staff as 'careers teacher'. The later report states that 95 per cent of schools recorded at least one member of staff with a major responsibility for careers. The statistical summaries provided in the two surveys are difficult to compare exactly, and it is difficult to assess whether more members of teaching staff have been designated careers teachers in the intervening period. Tables 5.1–5.2 give an indication of the numbers of staff involved in careers work at the time of the 1979 survey.

The real test of a school's commitment to careers work, however, is to assess what other responsibilities are given to those appointed Heads of Careers and to gain an indication of the time allowance given to them. Here interesting comparisons emerge. The later report shows that a higher proportion of Heads of Careers have 'careers' as their role responsibility — 44 per cent as opposed at 14 per cent in the earlier survey.

There is some evidence that schools and careers teachers are able to provide a quantitatively better service than they were in the early seventies. However, even though Heads of Careers may claim 'careers' as their sole responsibility, it does not mean that they are free of other teaching duties and many of them have a major subject teaching commitment outside their careers department. The 1979 report concludes: 'Heads of careers with no other responsibility were found to

Table 5.1. Provision of Teachers with Responsibility for Careers Education: By Size of School

Staffing provision	Size of School			All schools	
	0–600	601–1200	1201 or more	Numbers of schools	Percentages
One head of careers only	77	125	40	242	65
One head of careers and one or more deputies	4	41	19	64	17
Two heads of careers[1]	9	28	—	37	10
Three or more heads of careers[1]	—	5	4	9	2
No head of careers	11	4	3	18	5
All schools	101	203	66	370[2]	100

Notes: 1 Some of these heads of careers were assisted by one or more deputies.
2 Only 370 of the 384 sample schools could be used for this table.

Source: *Aspects of Secondary Education in England* (1979) HMI Report, London, HMSO. Reproduced by permission of the Controller, HMSO.

Table 5.2. Responsibilities of Heads of Careers

	Number of heads of careers	Percentages
Careers as the only responsibility	181	44
Careers as the first of two responsibilities	50	12
Careers as the second of two responsibilities	184	44
Total	415	100

Source: *Aspects of Secondary Education in England* (1979) HMI Report, London, HMSO. Reproduced by permission of the Controller, HMSO.

teach on average, for 28 periods in a 40 period week,' and that 'it was notable that there was an association between inadequate non-teaching time and poor careers guidance provision.' Where there may have been some developments in the appointment of staff to 'careers' work, the findings of the report lead one to question whether schools which appoint careers teachers are simply paying lip-service to the idea of careers without any real commitment of teacher time and financial resources.

What Do Careers Teachers Do?

The principal task of careers teachers is to help their students with the transition from school to what lies beyond. In practice this involves them in a wide range of activities outlined in Figure 5.3. In the main these activities centre around teaching a careers education curriculum principally to third, fourth and fifth year students, and the organization of a careers guidance programme which will involve other teaching staff, parents, employers and agencies, such as the Careers Service, in events such as parents' evenings, careers conventions and work experience schemes. These activities will involve considerable timetabling and administrative effort. One critical role is to maintain links with the local authority Careers Service, to provide an opportunity for Careers Officers to come into the school to interview pupils and to take part in careers programmes. Often this involves the preparation of school reports for those students having interviews with the Careers Officer, and in many cases the careers teacher's main administrative task

Figure 5.3. Activities Performed by Careers Teachers in Schools

Organization focused	• devising a careers programme throughout the school. • keeping other staff informed of the programme • liaising with teaching colleagues on the delivery of the careers education programme • arranging Careers Officer interviews • developing links with employer groups • organizing careers conventions • attending local careers organization meetings • developing record system and providing references for pupils
Client focused	• collecting and updating stocks of occupational information • carrying out individual helping interviews with pupils and parents • teaching careers education • organizing visits and work experience • administering occupational interest guides and computer aided guidance systems

will be to maintain a record system with details of pupils' careers interviews, interview notes, expected examination performance. Careers teachers are therefore centrally placed to prepare references for employers and other referral agencies.

Careers staff may well be involved in one-to-one interviewing with students, not for job placement, but for screening prior to the Careers Officer's visit or for referral to other agencies. Interviews in the fourth or fifth year may well be simply an opportunity to discuss a pupil's tentative career decisions or job choice and be concerned as much with education and personal issues as with those that are clearly vocational in nature.

Arguably, however, the most fundamental task of careers teachers is the provision and distribution of occupational information. In terms of the developmental model for school-based careers guidance outlined below, the acquisition, storage and distribution of careers information is the basic level at which careers work in schools operates. Its provision raises many questions about how accessible the information services can be made to students. Can careers information rooms remain open for school pupils, for example, at any time they choose to use them? The provision of careers information may also raise fundamental questions about the role of the careers teacher in school. For while most colleagues and students may see the careers teacher as the information expert on work, jobs and courses of study, careers teachers who see themselves largely as counsellors, coordinators or careers education specialists may well feel uncomfortable with a perception of their role which is solely that of the information specialist.

As several government reports have pointed out, resources for careers work vary considerably among schools. On average though, most secondary schools will have some of the resources outlined in Figure 5.4, with most schools providing a scale Head of Careers post with special responsibility for careers work, with other members of the teaching staff forming part of a careers team with a proportion of their time allocated to careers teaching or administration. In terms of physical resources, most schools will have some careers information provision occupying a specifically allocated careers information room or at least some library space. Most careers coordinators will also have their own office/interview room and, hopefully, a telephone.

Figure 5.4. *The Organization of Careers Work in Secondary Schools: An Example of Resource Provision*

Staffing: Careers department	Guidance: Structure of school	Physical resources	Outside contacts, agencies and resources
Head of careers with a team of two or three other teaching staff with responsibility for teaching part of the careers education programme. Input from year heads and sixth form tutor.	General pastoral care provided by year heads and form tutors. Possibility of involvement of full- or part-time counsellor.	Careers information room, containing printed and visual material Interview room. Classroom allocated for careers education.	LEA Careers Services. Employers/ professional bodies. Other educational institutions.

Having described the resources that are generally available for careers work in schools, it is important for us to acknowledge that different systems exist for preparing pupils for life after school. In some schools, particularly sixth form colleges or schools with a counsellor in post, there may well be a greater degree of emphasis on individual counselling than on careers education. In some schools the main emphasis will be a comprehensive single subject careers curriculum for all pupils with little in the way of one-to-one interviewing or counselling. In others; integrated guidance programmes, coordinated by year tutors and implemented in tutor groups throughout the school, may recognize the importance of parents, peer groups and community in helping students towards future personal and career development.

One way of examining the strengths of a particular school's careers programmes is to question how much help each individual pupil receives with career choice and the transition from school, because part of the problem of identifying the range of 'helping provision' is the interrelationship in most schools between functions which are exclusively to do with 'careers' and those to do with general pastoral care. For example, whilst many careers teachers may have the specific function of interviewing pupils about their career intentions, pupils may also refer their vocational concerns to teachers in a pastoral or welfare role, for example, form tutors and year heads. Additionally, if a school counsellor is in post, individual pupils may well refer themselves for individual counselling about personal, educational and vocational issues. Indeed, recent initiatives in encouraging greater tutorial work with students (Baldwin and Wells, 1980) are attempts to foster and encourage this kind of development; the team working under the Lancashire Active Tutorial project has developed a complete set of materials designed for use in tutorial periods, which have many of the objectives of careers education and address many of the issues discussed earlier under the heading of 'life skills'.

One useful way of conceptualizing the various kinds of school-based guidance provision is to draw a distinction between sources of specific help and expertise and those of a more general kind. According to Best *et al.* (1980), school-based guidance provision can best be seen as a matrix of helping interventions, which vary according to the immediate focus of the guidance and the degree of specialism of the helper. In the case of careers guidance, for example, the careers officer or careers coordinator is often the specialist helper, with subject teachers and year and form tutors likely to play a supportive role. In the case of educational and personal guidance, the school counsellor or educational psychologist may be seen as the specialist sources of help, to whom students can be referred. However, in solving routine welfare and educational problems it may be year heads and other tutors who play a predominant role in handling the majority of guidance issues.

The distinction between general and specialist practitioners may help to show the potential of all staff to share in the school guidance provision — a potential which is elaborated on later in the chapter. And while there may be some dispute as to whether pastoral care or guidance is the larger term, it has to be acknowledged that all teachers may have a potential role in assisting individual students with the transition from school to work or further training.

According to Watts and Fawcett (1980), however, there are problems inherent in tutor-based approaches to careers education, not least of which is the sense that some teachers may regard this extra focus to their form tutor role as an additional and largely unwanted task. There is, they argue, no substitute for a separate careers department with its special expertise, at the same time encouraging tutor group work with its emphasis on personal and social education.

Whatever the administrative context of careers work in schools, it is perhaps important to acknowledge, as previous research has shown, that home and community are powerful influences on achievement, level of aspiration and career choice. Indeed, there is a strong case to be made that school careers guidance should be based on a truly integrated approach; that students' experience at home and in the community should be carefully integrated with a 'whole-school' approach to the preparation of young people for life beyond school. As Law (1978) argues:

> Personal planning is, willy-nilly, caught up in a broad matrix of causes and consequences in the family, domestic, community and social life of the individual. What guidance and counselling seek to do is, therefore, interleaved for any individual student with a range of other 'guidance' experiences to be arbitrated by, and to arbitrate, what he experiences in professionally provided guidance experiences. It would be a 'delusion of grandeur' for guidance practitioners to imagine that they can or should accept sole responsibility for the guidance of young people. The contribution of professional guidance to the reality of guidance needs to be conceived in wholly other terms.

Some school-based careers practitioners would argue, of course, that this is what they have been doing anyway; others may see it as something of a threat to their cherished professional specialism. Whatever the case, an integrated careers guidance approach would seem to make substantial demands of careers teachers and counsellors in terms of organizational and networking skills and, as Law points out, this may not be easy for those careers practitioners who see their role primarily in terms of tutorial or counselling support with clients. In addition to administrative complexities of such an integrated approach, one could argue that the results could produce a diffused pattern of activity and approaches without a clearly identifiable focus, causing confusion for clients as well as consultants. On the positive side, it would seem to be an approach which could make institutions like schools and colleges more responsive to the guidance needs of individuals within it, and this potential outcome of an integrated approach is at the heart of the development model of careers guidance in schools proposed by Law and Watts (1977) and Law (1978b).

A Developmental Model for Careers Guidance in Schools

According to the model proposed by the above authors, the development of careers guidance systems within schools begins with the processing and display of occupational information (see Figure 5.5). This basic task has to be accomplished by someone in school; at an initial phase this may simply mean keeping and classifying occupational information in a filing cabinet. At a more advanced and sophisticated level, schools will provide a careers information room or resource centre, maintained by the careers coordinator, which is easily accessible

Figure 5.5. The Evolution of a School Careers Guidance Department: A Developmental Model.

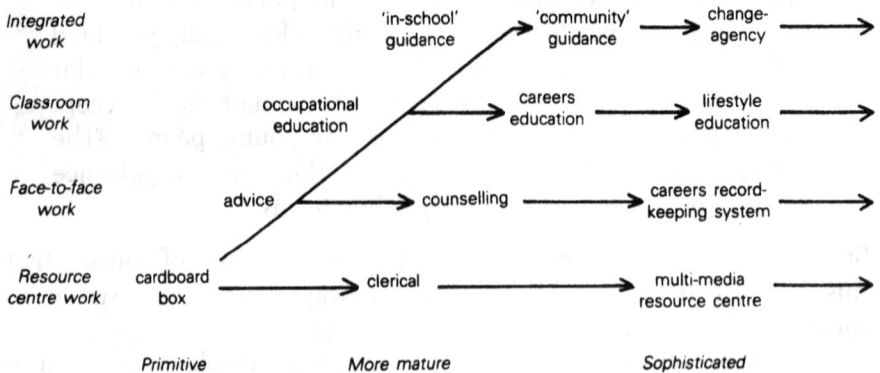

Source: B. Law (1977) Introduction to Careers Guidance, NICEC Training Module. Reproduced with the another's permission.

to all students and is resourced not only with printed occupational information but also with audio-visual materials.

A second setting of careers guidance work concerns face-to-face work with students, or the helping interview. At a basic level this could mean answering simple requests for information from students. At a more sophisticated level this could imply counselling interviews concerned with a thorough exploration of a client's values and aspirations — the development of work in this setting, making particular skill demands on the careers practitioner.

A third setting concerns the careers education curriculum. Most careers education programmes may, at a basic level, contain one or two talks about different occupations or a series of television or video programmes. At a more advanced level careers education can imply highly participative group discussion, facilitated sensitively by the careers practitioner, achieving many of the curriculum objectives described in more detail in an earlier chapter.

The fourth setting, which relates particularly to the idea of careers guidance taking place in an integrated setting, suggests ways in which careers coordinators may involve both school and community in preparing young people for the transition from school to work. Community-based work experience schemes, initiatives aimed at facilitating school-industry exchanges for teaching staff and employers and attempts to relate the whole curriculum to the world of work may involve the careers practitioner in a change-agency, catalytic role, in addition to those described earlier. Law (1978b) suggests that it is in this setting that major breakthroughs can take place in careers guidance work, since the whole school can be seen to play a part in the careers guidance provision and can presumably begin to pay serious attention to the career development of its pupils.

In reviewing the work of careers teachers in schools, it has to be acknowledged that a number of issues have dogged the development of careers education and guidance, particularly the refusal of many schools, *viz.* headteachers, to acknowledge the importance of this activity, or the methodological problems of implementing careers education successfully, the acquisition and organization of resources and the appointment of appropriate staff for the work.

Two principal problems remain to be resolved before school-based careers education can be developed further. Firstly, there needs to be a clearer consensus between local authorities and their schools about the need for careers education and what they are trying to achieve in its name. A recent survey by Law showed that, in those authorities that had a policy on careers education and guidance in their schools, wide differences in meaning were attributed to the term 'careers education'. For some it implied developing school-industry links; for others it implied increasing commitment to all forms of personal and social education. Only when a clear consensus emerges will it be possible to identify exactly the roles that careers teachers need to fulfil and the criteria according to which people are appointed to the work.

Secondly, more attention will have to be paid to the question of in-service training for careers teachers. While many schools now have scale posts for careers coordinators, careers education and guidance is hardly ever a component of courses of initial training of teachers. Most teachers therefore find themselves appointed to posts of responsibility for careers work without any form of training. As Heap (TES, 3 September 1982) observes:

> ... the role of the careers teachers is often regarded as non-educational. Its traditions lie in the work of well intentioned amateurs whose experience of life outside the classroom was often quite limited and whose opinions were often very biased, but who believed that some form of guidance was better than no guidance at all.

It is to be hoped in future that newly trained teachers will have an increased awareness of what can be achieved in their personal and tutorial roles and therefore be more able to undertake work within a careers team. However, the problem of training remains and while resources for in-service and post-experience training of careers teachers remain scarce, there will be no effective training for teaching staff appointed to this key role.

Careers Services in Higher Education

In terms of student numbers, the higher education system in the UK has almost trebled in size since 1960. In the decade following the publication of the Robbins Report the output of university graduates doubled and this growth continues. In 1973, 52,856 university students graduated from universities in the United Kingdom (this figure excludes those in medicine, dentistry and veterinary science). In 1983 this figure is likely to be 68,913 — a growth in output of 30 per cent even in the last ten years. In the period 1975–81 the output of graduates from polytechnics has risen by 49 per cent from 10,473 to 20,532. This pattern of growth is, however, unlikely to continue into the second half of the decade, because the recent growth in student numbers largely reflects demographic trends and increases in the size of the 18-year-old age group, rather than any dramatic increase in the participation rates of those qualified to enter the higher education system. Also, cuts in higher education expenditure will mean a contraction in the number of student places, even though the demand for places may well increase. However, the figures do seem to show why graduate employment is the 'problem' now that it was not in the fifties and sixties and also help to explain and account for the sizeable development of careers advisory services in higher education institutions. For every university and polytechnic in the country now has full-time careers advisory or counselling staff to cater for the vocational counselling needs of students.

The development of careers advisory services in higher education began in the immediate post-war period with the establishment of university appointments boards, which, as the name implied, provided final year students with advice about employment and graduate placement service. By 1967 a Standing Conference of University Careers Services (SCUAS) was formed and two years later membership was opened to polytechnics and Scottish central institutions. With increasingly wide membership and an acknowledgment of a counselling and advisory as well as a placement role, SCUAS changed its name to the Association of Graduate Careers Advisory Services in 1977 — an association of constituent careers and counselling services in universities, polytechnics and colleges of higher education with over 400 individual members.

At the heart of this cohesive professional grouping is a country-wide information gathering and information distribution network facilitated by a Central Services Unit, whose full-time staff have the task of distributing graduate vacancy information, publishing occupational information sheets (which are, incidentally, written collaboratively by AGCAS members), as well as maintaining a register of graduate employers and publishing statistical summaries of graduate employment data for both universities and polytechnics. The size and scope of this information network, owned by subscriber careers services rather than an external agency or independent publishers, make it without doubt the major information resource on which individual careers services draw and clearly distinguish the activities of careers advisory services in higher education from those in other parts of the educational system. Unlike other large professional groupings, AGCAS has no full-time secretariat, but relies on individual members to take up key coordinating roles. A committee and working party structure ensure that issues of special interest to counsellors, such as sex equality, schools liaison and information gathering, are developed further. AGCAS, under the auspices of its Training Sub-Committee, provides all its own training courses and programmes. A further example of the partnership and collaboration which exist between AGCAS member services is provided by the Mutual Aid Scheme, in which graduates of one institution, whether university, polytechnic or college of higher education, can seek vocational counselling help and information from another AGCAS institution if they need to.

The success of this information sharing amongst AGCAS member services and the considerable degree of collaboration and cooperation which exists between them can, in part, be explained by the energy and enthusiasm of individual careers advisers. Part of the success may also be to do with the nature of the employment opportunities faced by their clients. The graduate employment market is a fairly recognizable entity and careers counsellors acquire specialized knowledge in understanding its complexities. In addition, it is perfectly possible for AGCAS members to consult with their confrères in the Standing Conference of Employers of Graduates to estimate for a given year the number of vacancies and training opportunities which are likely to occur in the light of the expected graduate output from the higher education system. They are therefore able to provide a rough estimate of employment trends on a national basis, which is not possible for other sectors of the labour market, both because the major graduate recruiters are able to predict in advance the nature of their graduate recruitment and because the graduate level of entry to employing organizations is well defined.

How Do Careers Services in Higher Education Operate?

Careers counselling agencies in higher education vary considerably in size, staffing and methodology. Fundamentally, however, they all attempt to provide an occupational information and helping interview service to the final year student population, whether this consists of first degree, postgraduate or diploma students. Most services also try to provide a limited placement service for those about to graduate, even if this simply means letting students know where job vacancies are likely to occur.

In the larger careers services a number of careers advisers (a ratio of one careers adviser to 400 final year students is not uncommon) see student clients on a self-referral basis, often starting in the second year of study. In addition, a careers information officer and secretarial staff also form part of the careers advisory service. Staffing levels, however, vary tremendously, not always in line with the size of the institution which the careers centres serve. The financing and funding of services also vary. In the university sector all services are funded by the universities themselves and staff are employees on conditions which are closer to those of administrative than of academic staff. In polytechnics funding and staffing are on different bases. In some polytechnics the careers counselling services are funded by the institution, with counsellors and advisers accorded status equivalent to academic teaching staff. In a number of cases the local authority careers service provides a service to polytechnic students, by siting specialist Careers Officers on the particular polytechnic campus in the local authority area. As a general rule, careers counselling arrangements in colleges of higher education follow the polytechnic pattern.

These differences in staffing and funding are also reflected in variations in practice and underlying philosophy, so that the notion of a shared professional view amongst careers advisers in higher education is often difficult to sustain. Some careers services still put a good deal of effort into information giving and placement activities, while others incline more to one-to-one counselling work with students. Yet again, some services, of which Keele University is perhaps the most obvious example (Newsome *et al.*, 1973), refuse to distinguish between vocational counselling issues and those of general student counselling, and therefore have an integrated counselling service for students so that students can refer themselves at any stage of their course to discuss educational and emotional issues as well as those to do with vocational choice and decision making. (A number of polytechnic services have also adopted the Keele model.)

In some services careers advisers may specialize according to the needs of a particular client group and see students from two or three different courses. Similarly, some careers advisers specialize according to a particular occupational area, for example, teaching, so that all students expressing an interest in a given occupational area are referred to one particular individual adviser or counsellor. The job titles themselves suggest the wide variety of role definitions: 'Appointments Officer', 'Careers Adviser', 'Careers Counsellor', 'Student Counsellor' indicate differing styles and assumptions about the needs of the student clients and, implicitly, about an adviser's own professional practice.

Despite these differences, some generalizations can be made about the way careers services in higher education operate. They all offer students the chance of at least one 'careers' interview lasting up to an hour, backed up by access to extensive occupational information services. Many careers services now have computerized guidance

127

systems (see Chapter 4) and have in the past used measures of occupational interest. The main thrust of their placement work is the annual 'milk round' during which the major graduate recruiters visit university and polytechnic campuses to interview final year students. Most services also provide a vacancy mailing service to former students. The follow-up of former students is carried out assiduously in order to provide highly accurate data about the employment of recent graduates.

The steady deterioration in the graduate employment market since 1981 and the increasing number of clients have meant some innovative changes in the way careers services organize their work. Workshops, sometimes residential, for unemployed graduates are now a common feature of the work of some services. Developments in careers education (see Chapter 2), as a result of which careers advisers are likely to see students in group discussion sessions, often in the context of their courses of study, are putting careers advisers increasingly in a group tutor/facilitator role. At the same time, recent cuts in university expenditure have resulted in some cases in dramatic reductions in the staffing of careers services in higher education; this, too, is forcing careers advisers to review their working practices to respond to increasing pressures both for themselves and their clients. While it is difficult to predict what effect these changes will have on the future viability of these student services, it is possible to point to past successes. For although there has been little evaluatory research on the effectiveness of careers services in higher education, it seems that they have been generally successful in responding to the needs of their immediate client group. The reasons for this success are probably to do with a number of features of their role and the clearly marketed transition services they offer to students.

Firstly, unlike local authority careers advisers, careers advisers in higher education are largely institution-based. This enables them to maintain important institutional networks with teaching staff and at the same time understand fully the educational experience of their clients as well as help them with their search for a vocational identity. The potential for understanding a client's personal, educational and career development is therefore greater than for those guidance services based outside educational institutions which deal with 'crisis' counselling. Secondly, the specialized and singular nature of the graduate employment market allows services to provide both counselling and placement services to students simultaneously and therefore to appeal to a broad cross-section of the student population. A third and related reason for success is that graduates in the main acknowledge that the services provided by their own graduating institution are likely to be better equipped to meet the vocational counselling and placement needs of recent graduates than state or private placement agencies.

Careers Counselling Services for Adults

It seems an unhappy irony that at a time of a major industrial upheaval, characterized by increasing rates of redundancy and job change, there is no effective national provision of careers counselling services for adults. Since the closure of the Occupational Guidance Units in 1980, local education authorities have, in the main, lacked both the political will and financial resources to extend their services to the adult population. It is therefore left to the private fee-charging careers and vocational guidance agencies to fill this vacuum and extend their services.

In reviewing the provision of careers counselling services for adults, it is perhaps worth reflecting on the role of the Occupational Guidance Units, which were disbanded as a cost cutting exercise by the government in June 1980. The Occupational Guidance Units (OGUs) were established in 1966 to offer occupational guidance to anyone over 18, at any occupational level, whether they were employed or not. They provided individual vocational counselling, often aided by measures of occupational interest and aptitude, and reviewed a client's education and training opportunities as well as those concerned with immediate employment. There were forty-three OGUs situated throughout the country, employing some 365 civil servants in the Manpower Services Commission. The regional centres provided a national service to adults in need of occupational information and counselling and in 1979/80 they catered for some 50,000 clients. As the first complete function to be cut by the Department of Employment, the OGUs were thought to be too expensive a facility to maintain, with the MSC arguing that Job Centres and Job Libraries could meet the needs of the clients previously catered for by the Occupational Guidance Units. Whether employment advisers in Job Centres provide the same or even a similar service to that provided by the more extensively trained staff of the OGUs is open to question. They may well be able to impart immediate advice concerning employment opportunities and job vacancies, but it seems clear that the state employment services regard any form of in-depth vocational counselling as an expensive luxury.

The careers counselling agencies in the private sector, not surprisingly, still flourish. This small number of profit and non-profit making agencies, largely based in London, caters for clients of all ages, not just adults, and charges fees according to the kind of service offered. Staffed largely by occupational psychologists, they provide a diagnostic vocational guidance service, based on the use of psychometric tests and appraisal interviews and reports. Their approach is unashamedly 'talent-matching', and they see it as their task to provide a 'recommended occupation' or course of action to their clients. Typically a full consultation will consist of the client completing a half-day of psychometic tests, probably of personality, interest and aptitude, followed by a consultation interview lasting up to two hours. Finally, a report is typed and on the basis of the personality profile, statement of occupational interests and vocational aptitudes, as well as the summary of the interview, and a recommendation is then given. As one would expect, a different approach is provided according to the age of the client. An interview with a school leaver may be as much concerned with educational counselling as with vocational counselling; adults in mid-career may well prefer to seek a career development interview rather than undertake an extensive range of psychometic tests.

In assessing the work of the private vocational guidance agencies, a number of points emerge which distinguish them from other services in the educational sector. Firstly, the time spent on each client is considerable, often the equivalent of a whole day. Secondly, there is little attempt to provide any kind of placement service alongside the vocational counselling. Finally, they collude with the notion that there is but one 'right' occupation for each individual as long as it can be properly diagnosed.

At the beginning of this chapter it was stated that vocational counselling is essentially an educational enterprise undertaken by educational institutions and there is every indication that this will continue to be the case. For in reviewing the development of careers guidance services in this country, one trend in particular can be discerned. The longer students stay in education or training beyond school leaving age and postpone entry to work, the more likely it is that careers counselling becomes an enterprise undertaken by educational institutions rather than state employment services. In her international review, Reubens concludes that in both West Germany and the United Kingdom:

> New organisational forms have been created to reduce the responsibilities of the guidance personnel of the employment service toward young people still in educational institutions, substituting either a joint organisation or personnel located in the school system or attached to it. More activities are located in schools, especially counselling about the occupational implications of educational choices.

Even where guidance has been largely an enterprise of state employment agencies, for example, in West Germany, there is a growth in the development of school- or college-based careers counselling activities and programmes. It seems likely that in this country in secondary, further and higher education, careers counselling services will continue to form a bridge between the educational sector and the wider employment market and that careers counsellors will continue to provide the key function of helping students of whatever age with the transition from education to work.

For adults facing mid-career change, for those workers who face redundancy or further retraining, there exist no effective counselling services. National provision in this crucial field is, it seems, sadly lacking.

Chapter 6

Community Resources

As we saw in an earlier chapter, family and community exert a powerful influence on the career aspirations of young people. The influence of factors such as social class and family background on occupational choice is well documented (Maizels, 1970). More recently, Fogelman (1979), reporting on the results of the National Child Development Study of career aspirations of 16-year-olds, acknowledged that adolescents' aspirations are related to their own and their teachers' expectations, but concluded:

> we have confirmed using a large and nationally representative sample, the strong relationship found by other researchers between future [career] plans and the background variables such as social class and parental education.

The theme is reiterated by Willis (1976) in his study of the influence of peer group culture in a Midlands school: 'In terms of actual "job choice", it is the "lads" culture and not the official careers material which provides the most located and deeply influential guide for the future.'

Class culture and family background are, therefore, major determinants of the aspirations and the kinds of work entered by young people. These and similar previous research findings may at first seem to put into question the fundamental rationale of many careers advisory services whose main aim is to exhort clients to make rational and autonomous career decisions in the light of their own individual aspirations and abilities. New initiatives, however, on the part of local authority careers services represent an attempt to build on, rather than deny, the influence of family and community on the aspiration level of their children. Courses on 'careers' for parents are, for example, one way of acknowledging the powerful cultural processes operating on young people and attempt to incorporate parents in the guidance process. Careers advisers and counsellors are not denied a role, but have a significant one in developing greater awareness amongst parents of the opportunity structure and of the ways young people can be supported in the transition from school to work. The task for the careers practitioner now becomes one of supplementing and coordinating all the resources of the community to provide effective guidance programmes rather than working in isolation from them.

There is, of course, nothing new in the idea of involving parents and community in a careers guidance programme. Talks by visiting speakers, registers of parents willing to act as 'careers consultants' and school or college careers conventions are all opportunities to invite people outside an educational institution to take part in its careers guidance activities. In the case of careers conventions, for example, representatives from local employers, professional bodies and training agencies are invited to be on hand to answer questions from pupils facing career decisions. A convention provides a highly structured opportunity for young people to ask questions of adults outside of family and school, which may begin to help them decide on the route they take through the opportunity and training structure. For the most part, however, events such as these are primarily given over to basic information giving and therefore provide a limited opportunity for learning about the world of work. It is likely, for example, that students will obtain a clearer idea of entry and training requirements, but less likely that they will get answers to such questions as, 'would I be good at this kind of work?', or 'what's it really like to do this job with your company?' The opportunity for personal feedback about career plans and potential is limited.

Attempts at linking school curricula to commercial and industrial problems, which involve pupils in practical projects work by visiting local firms and talking to people already at work, are probably more effective at giving pupils a more realistic sense of what work is like. (This is certainly true of students on sandwich courses in further and higher education.) Many of these attempts to bridge school life and work life and provide young people with an increased sense of the demands of working life and the skills which are important in the work place are highlighted in *Schools and Working Life* (DES, 1981).

In reviewing guidance programmes, the main aim of this chapter is two-fold. Firstly, it explores the ways in which the community can be involved in the guidance activity of a school to provide pupils with an increased sense of their own worth and potential, together with an understanding of life beyond school. Secondly, it sets out to describe examples of coordinated community-based programmes designed to help young people find and retain jobs, using as volunteers ordinary working people — generalist rather than specialist helpers — to provide help, advice and support. In doing so, it begins to examine the claim that guidance can be a community enterprise, rather than an activity which is exclusively left to helping professionals: careers teachers, counsellors and careers advisers.

The relationship between school and community in promoting guidance activity is examined in detail by Law and Watts (1977). Their analysis of six secondary schools and their careers education programmes sought to show the extent to which the resources of school and community could be brought together to provide effective programmes concerned with the preparation of students for life beyond school. The authors question much of the value and effectiveness of traditional careers guidance activity. They cite numerous examples of programmes and events which suggest that on paper student needs are being met, when in reality a gulf exists between the client need and the school guidance provision. The careers convention to which pupils are allowed a thirty-five minute attendance with no preparation or follow-up work on the part of the teacher, and the tutorial programme which is alleged to be concerned with social and careers education and is concerned largely with registers and prayers, are two obvious examples. Even when the school careers information resources are adequate, it seems, students fail to use them effectively, if there is an inefficient careers education programme operating within the school. The authors conclude that to provide a viable careers guidance programme it is important to marshal resources both within the school and in the work community if students are to be helped with occupational choice, decision-making and work entry. Guidance should and can be a community enterprise. This has implications for the careers teacher:

> ... Such a notion assigns to the professional a harder rather than an easier task, for it means that the guidance role needs to work essentially by transgressing the school's boundary structure.... Within such a conception the professional becomes not merely a source of guidance but also a facilitator of multifarious other sources, many of which will have important careers education functions to play.

and for the school: 'The school has high social centrality and is strategically well-placed to act as facilitator and co-ordinator of a regained communal responsibility for its young.'

From their study it seems clear that the most important implication of linking the resources of the wider community to the existing careers guidance provisions in educational settings concerns effective coordination. Careers teachers and careers advisers trained primarily in one-to-one interviewing and careers education will require a new range of skills in coordinating programmes and events. Negotiating with outside agencies, linking people across institutional boundaries and managing groups of people require the communication and entrepreneurial skills associated with sales and management occupations rather than with teaching and counselling; yet these are precisely the skills required to achieve effective coordination. Nowhere is this more apparent than in the planning and provision of work experience schemes and programmes, which may be characterized by a number of different stages:

1 deciding on the aims and scope of the project — in terms of the year group with which it is to take place, the length and timing of the work experience placement.
2 enlisting the support of teaching colleagues — many of whom may be involved in visiting students while they are on placement, and the parents of those taking part;
3 preparing students for their placement during tutor periods or careers education sessions;
4 identifying employers who may be able to offer placements;
5 ensuring that the programme is monitored;
6 arranging for formal feedback from pupils and employers, the results of which are then circulated to teachers and parents.

Organizing work experience can require a considerable degree of coordination but, as the following case studies attempt to show, the participation of employers, parent teachers associations and trade unionists supported by the local authority careers service is likely to generate considerable interest and involvement in the careers guidance process. A coordinated approach to guidance is therefore likely to have considerable pay-offs for both careers practitioners and students.

Perhaps the most obvious way in which community help can be enlisted for a school's careers guidance programme is in the provision of work experience for pupils. Generally, work experience in this country which is school based, provides fourth and fifth year pupils with a chance to sample one kind of work for a week or more on employers' premises. Administrative arrangements vary, but it is usually the task of the Head of Careers or careers coordinator to enlist the support of local employers to provide suitable work experience placements and to match these with the expressed interests of the students. A student's progress is often monitored, and reports sent from the employer to the school, and students have a chance to write about and discuss their experiences in classroom-based sessions. The organization of school-based work experience programmes in particular requires the support and involvement of parents, employers, teaching staff and, of course, the students themselves. It is clearly a community enterprise, relying as it does on the cooperation of the school, industry and parents in a particular geographical area.

Some of the features and possible benefits of work experience are listed in Figure 6.1. In most cases work experience schemes are carefully planned and a considerable amount of preparation is usually required to make it a period of structured learning. In the case of students at school, work experience allows them to take on the temporary status of 'worker' rather than 'student' and therefore demands a far greater degree of involvement than works visits or work observation. In addition, most students are allowed their own choice of the kind of placement they wish to undertake, and this tends to ensure a high degree of commitment. As a result it is not surprising that work

Figure 6.1. Work Experience

Features	Possible benefits
Provides first-hand experience of work and skill sampling.	Encourages greater self-confidence and maturity. Increases motivation.
Promotes an awareness of the structure of local industries and services and possibilities for employment.	Increases opportunity awareness.
Provides adult role models.	Increases students' social skills, particularly in relating to adults.
Gives insight into the rituals of the work place, in particular the 'psycho-social' aspects of work.	Eases the transition from school to work.
Allows student to sample different work environments.	Develops vocational identity and facilitates career decision-making by encouraging self-awareness and providing occupational information.
Puts students in contact with recruiting employers.	Job placement can be easier, as it is for sandwich students in further and higher education.
Requires participation by employers and teaching staff.	Improves school-industry and community links.

experience schemes generally meet with success. Allowing young pupils to experience work at first hand is generally seen to increase self-confidence, to give insights into the meaning of work and to develop skills and competencies which help with career decision-making.

School-Based Work Experience Programmes

The different forms of school-based work experience are summarized by Watts (1983) and Eggleston (1982). In some areas of the country programmes are administered centrally in a local education authority with a work experience coordinator, often provided by the local authority careers service. In other areas individual schools compete for what seems like a shrinking number of placements. In other areas, too, an outside agency such as Project Trident organizes the schemes for schools who wish to participate. There are advantages to both types of system: on the one hand, economy of effort in schemes which are centrally coordinated, and, on the other, the chance for individual schools and colleges to develop close links with their own local employers. It seems that over a third of secondary schools offer work experience to some of their pupils. Commonly this takes the form of a week's placement for fifth year pupils. As Jamieson (1972) points out, students from low ability groups are often the first to take part in and benefit from work experience, and there is evidence that the most able pupils are least likely to take part, presumably because pupils' parents or teachers see work experience as concerned largely with entry to work rather than a learning experience in its own right.

There is therefore a tendency for pupils who see themselves remaining in education until age 21+ to exempt themselves from work experience schemes. The development of Brighton's Pre-Employment Project described later in this chapter lends further support to this analysis.

Why is work experience provision gaining in popularity? Apart from the perceived benefits to those taking part, there seem to be two reasons why school-based work experience seems set for further de-velopment, despite the apparent difficulty in finding placements. Firstly, work experience is often a substitute for timetable careers education. If a careers teacher or careers coordinator has difficulty in negotiating timetable time for careers work, it is often easier to ask for, but not necessarily to administer, a work experience programme. At least some of the career needs of some of the pupils will be met in this way, and the careers teacher faced with the problem of lack of resources will be able to demonstrate that 'careers' work is taking place. Logistically, too, it provides one way of introducing 'careers' into the timetable, since the work experience scheme itself will require considerable preparation and follow-up. The danger in this approach is that the whole of a careers teacher's time will be spent administering a scheme of this kind, with little time and energy spent on the provision of careers information, interviewing or careers education. There is also a second reason why work experience has developed so successfully and that is to do with promoting school/industry and community links. At their best, work experience programmes can represent a tangible attempt to make the organization of a school more open to outside influence. Work experience can require the support of the entire school organization — many teachers, for example, may be involved in visiting students on their placements — and at the same time it invites the cooperation of parents and employers, thereby generating a great deal of potential for goodwill between school and community and establishing school/industry links.

If work experience has been successful from an organizational point of view, there is unfortunately little research evidence to support the claims made for it. As Watts (1983) points out, objective research on the results for individual learning of school-based work experience remains thin on the ground. Much of the rationale for work experience rests on the largely positive reported feedback from students and employers. Black (1976), in a survey of 700 pupils who had taken part in Project Trident, found that 91 per cent had found the experience both useful and enjoyable. Of the employers surveyed, 88 per cent thought that the job had been appropriate to the pupil's abilities and only 3 per cent reported that any real problems had arisen. Of the parents surveyed, 80 per cent thought that the pupils' confidence about starting work had increased and none thought that it had decreased. Significantly, there was no evidence that work experience would distract pupils from their school work: 66 per cent seemed more able to acquire academic qualifications. Overall, 89 per cent of the parents said they would recommend other parents to encourage their children to have such experience.

In a study which centred on the effects on those taking part, Pumfrey and Schofield (1982) attempted to test the effect of work experience on pupil's career maturity. They administered the Crites Career Maturity Inventory to eighty fifth year pupils and found that work experience had a statistically significant effect on three of the six aspects of the career maturity test: Attitudes, Self-Appraisal and Occupational Knowledge. Although the study encountered certain methodological difficulties, principally to do with the use of an American test with British students, their results suggest that school-based work experience had a significant and positive effect on the career maturity of those taking part.

If, as Watts argues, there is little research evidence to support the success of work experience, there seems to be no doubt that students themselves consider it extremely useful. It is clear, for example, from the survey carried out by Keil (1976) of school leavers' attitudes to the way school had prepared them for work, that those interviewed saw the provision of work experience as the most useful way in which they could be prepared for the transition from school to work. Of nearly 500 comments received from interviews with young people, 31 per cent were concerned with work visits and experience of employment. The remainder of the results are detailed in Table 6.1.

Table 6.1. Replies to Question: How Do You Think Schools Should Prepare Young People for Work? (294 interviews, 489 comments)

Comments	Comments (%) given by 150 male respondents		Comments (%) given by 144 female respondents		All comments	
1 More visits, experience of employment	82	(31)	72	(32)	154	(31)
2 More visits of people at work to schools	45	(17)	31	(14)	76	(16)
3 More 'realistic' advice	63	(24)	59	(26)	122	(25)
4 More time for 'careers' discussions	55	(21)	58	(25)	113	(23)
5 'An impossible task', 'Can't do anything'	7	(3)	2	(1)	9	(2)
6 Other replies	9	(3)	6	(3)	15	(3)
	261	(99)	228	(101)	489	(100)

Source: E.T. Keil (1976).

Post-School Work Experience

Work experience has been the central element of the government's measures for the young unemployed. Since the introduction of job creation schemes in the mid-1970s, central government, by way of the Manpower Services Commission, has given priority to keeping unemployed young people occupied with some form of temporary work experience or training. Both unions and employers, however, resisted the idea of creating 'artificial' jobs, and job creation as a solution to youth unemployment was subsequently abandoned. Temporary experience of work was an altogether more acceptable proposition, particularly if it was related to skill training and coupled with further education. Work experience, therefore, became the major element of the Youth Opportunities Programme, accounting for 84 per cent of all places in 1980/81. Of the various kinds of work experience scheme: Community Service, Training Workshops, Project-Based, and Work Experience in Employers' Premises, the last (WEEP) accounted for the major share, with 67 per cent of the work experience places offered, with trainees given up to six months' work experience with a single employer.

However, the provision of work experience placements under YOP has not gone without criticism; in particular, allegations that placements of this kind are a form of cheap labour and simply substitutions for 'real' jobs abound. Even the MSC's own research suggests that some 30 per cent of employers providing placements are substituting WEEP trainees for regular and permanent employees, which is perhaps not surprising given that the majority of places are provided by small, non-unionized employers where there is a history of exploitation. Large organizations have, by and large, not provided the number of places expected of them. Furthermore, the expectation that a YOP work experience placement might lead to full-time permanent employment for those taking part has not been fulfilled. In 1980, 32 per cent of those leaving WEEP schemes found permanent employment. The figure for those leaving project-based work experience was lower still, at 21 per cent. At the outset, 70 per cent of YOP trainees found permanent employment.

Despite this, WEEP and other work experience schemes have been successful in providing some form of experience of work to thousands of young people and have provided them with a chance to learn some skills and to keep them from the unemployment register. Perhaps this is the most important distinction to be drawn between school-based work experience and that provided under the Youth Training Scheme. At school work experience is seen largely as an educational supplement, designed to help pupils make career decisions. Under YOP and YTS work experience is seen as a substitute for permanent paid employment. An early study by Gregory and Rees (1978) tried to assess the benefits of the then Work Experience

Programme. While the majority of those taking part had positive feelings about the scheme and agreed that they had gained some limited skills, there was no evidence to suggest that the trainees had enhanced their job aspirations or expectations. The authors, however, acknowledged that any benefits that were derived from the scheme were largely due to the existing employees. They concluded, 'The great strength of the scheme lay in the commitment we found amongst key individuals at the factory and in the general support for the scheme given by the ordinary workforce.'

Both school-based and post-school work experience provide students with a chance to learn occupational skills in a real working environment. For those on WEEP, it also increases the possibility of finding permanent full-time employment often arising directly from the work experience placement. It also provides a chance for participants to increase their self-awareness in relation to work and to increase occupational knowledge.

Arguably, however, one of the main reasons for the success of work experience arises from the contact between sutdents and adults in the work place and the potential for learning that this contact affords. Adult workers can provide support to those on work experience and useful contacts which may be helpful in job search. More importantly, they can give useful feedback to work experience 'trainees' and act as vital role models in helping young people achieve independence and maturity in the process of adjustment to working life. School-based work experience in particular can be seen as a part of a broader guidance provision to help young people in the transition from school to work. It represents a coordinated attempt to provide experience-based learning which takes place outside the educational institution and relies on considerable community support. If, as seems likely, the community becomes a base for much post-education training and temporary work (community workshops, community industry and community programmes all provide evidence of this activity), it also seems likely that 'community' will be a key theme in the delivery of careers guidance, in particular with the transition to full-time employment.

The four case studies which follow attempt to show how careers guidance in its broadest sense can be a community enterprise undertaken by specialist teachers and careers practitioners and generalist helpers (working adults). They share a number of common characteristics.

1 They are all examples of planned programmes designed to help young people achieve worker status. They are all concerned

with enhancing the personal and career development of those taking part, whether they are pupils at school, students in higher education or the young unemployed.

2   All four schemes require planned, central coordination, aimed at bringing together people and resources, often working across institutional boundaries and formal organization structures. All four draw their success from the principle of networking.

3   They all rely on the voluntary involvement and active participation of older workers who act as supporting agents for the young clients. These generalist helpers are often the informal teachers and counsellors to the client group.

4   Three of the four examples use group participation and group discussion as a way of consolidating the experience and learning of those taking part.

The first two case studies are concerned with nationally known projects, which are entirely community-based and take place outside educational settings. Both rely on the principal of 'outreach' in trying to work with clients in a way which the statutory agencies find difficult and, while they employ central coordinators, most of the client contact is carried out by generalist voluntary helpers. Both the Grubb Institute's TWL Network and Capital Radio Jobmate are concerned with a similar client group — the young unemployed in urban areas. The second two case studies are on a smaller scale and drawn from local experience, and both operate from educational settings, with 'specialist' coordinators.

The Working Coach

Like the Capital Radio Jobmate Scheme, the Working Coach concept developed by Bazalgette relies on the active participation of ordinary working people in giving guidance to school leavers and young workers. Unlike Jobmate, however, the Working Coach idea was developed initially to help young people with transition and adjustment to working life rather than to provide help primarily with job search or unemployment counselling.

Arising from Bazalgette's (1978) research in Coventry, which examined many of the crucial issues in the transition from school to work, the Working Coach was seen as someone with experience of shopfloor work, who had both a concern for the welfare and development of young people and an ability to relate to young workers, and who would be allowed time off from normal employment to carry out weekly tutorial/discussion work with a small group of workers from different backgrounds. The key features of the programme envisaged by Bazalgette were:

1 To create groups of young employees of about twelve to fourteen members each. They would be of different ages, preferably with different lengths of experience of work, and not all working for the same firm.
2 To allocate to each group an industrial coach who would normally be an experienced shopfloor employee who would carry tutorial responsibility for his group, or similar adult. Occasionally a coach might come from a school or college but this would be the exception rather than the rule.
3 Each group would meet at regular intervals, say once a week for a whole day, in a setting which is not a usual educational one, but which has associations with the work place, for example, a works canteen or conference room.

The industrial or Working Coaching scheme would, according to Bazalgette, provide greater stability for young workers, enable young workers to learn with adults on an experiential rather than didactic basis and, finally, help young people's personal and career development. The scheme would also prove valuable learning for the coaches themselves and provide a stimulus for their own personal development.

With the rise of youth unemployment, much of the subsequent development of the Working Coach idea has been with young unemployed. Units have now been established in a number of parts of the country: North London, Wolverhampton and Glasgow, as part of the Grubb Institute's TWL Network, with the aim of encouraging young people to interact with the working world and helping them in their search for work. Pupils about to leave school and those already unemployed can attend TWL workshops, which consist of six to ten young people meeting regularly with their Working Coach along the lines already indicated. Evaluatory studies show that those taking part have been actively encouraged in their search for work and have maintained their motivation for work itself. Research carried out with a sample of 190 young people showed that they divided into three groups:

1 TWL change (55 per cent): those who reported their TWL Workshop had made a significant difference to them and for whom there was evidence of this in their relations to the world outside;

2   no TWL change (38 per cent): those who reported no change, or for whom change was confined to behaviour in the Workshop itself;

3   inclusive (7 per cent): a small group who felt the Workshop had helped, but could not identify any specific change in attitudes or behaviour.

In assessing further the value of the Working Coach model, three points seem to emerge (Reed, 1980; Armstrong *et al.*, 1981). Firstly, in helping young people in the transition from school to work and the adoption of adult status, generalist helpers — ordinary working adults — are every bit as important as the specialist teachers and careers officers. In some senses, the authors argue, the generalist can be even more successful than the specialist in helping young people achieve adult status:

> ... it was apparent to us that in the process of becoming adult, young people often felt diminished or patronized because of the predominantly specialist approach from adults. Many young people subsequently told us that prior to taking part in the project they had never experienced the generalist approach from adults. When they left school they were being extruded from the sociological role of childhood, but their actual encounters with adults to that point hindered them from taking up the psychological role of adult which was essential if they were to cope with the problems of finding a job.

Secondly, the development of the idea of the Working Coach was, it seems, the first step towards the recognition that guidance could be a shared community enterprise which depended on local networks. Reed *et al.* (1982) provide a vivid account of the energy which was released during the TWL Network Project:

> ... in establishing its three regional bases TWL needed to operate across the boundaries of industry and commerce, education, guidance, social and community services. The extent to which this triggered off a chain reaction of responses surprised the staff. It seems that natural linkages between different members of a community and its institutions were being reactivated and brought alive. Young people discovered a wider range of resources available to them in negotiating and making their way in that community and saw new links between resources

and opportunities. Other members of the community involved with TWL were able to see how they could contribute in ways which they had previously discounted or resisted.

Finally, in operating across institutional boundaries of school, work and community, the TWL network was in itself activating community networks; as a result it released potential for change and was providing young people with a greater degree of access to community resources. Given the economic and employment climate in this country in the last four years, it was critically important, the authors argue, to recreate this sense of community membership in giving some support to the young unemployed in particular.

> ... TWL was based on the confidence that young people had the capacity to take control of their own lives, but were often unaware of it; and that ordinary working adults had the capacity to activate this natural process and to maintain it, but like the young people, they were either unaware of that capacity, or did not know how to use it.

Capital Radio Jobmate

Capital Jobmate is a London-based project, sponsored by the National Extension College in association with Capital Radio and financed by the Manpower Services Commission. The aim of the project is to help unemployed young people find and maintain work by using local radio, a telephone referral system and an informal network of community-based Jobmates — adults from all walks of life, who give their time on a voluntary basis. It was designed initially to help all those unemployed young people who were not using the 'specialist' services provided by job centres, careers services and other helping agencies.

The project has its origins in another, similar pilot project based in the West Country, entitled 'Just the Job'. By 'phoning a free-phone service linked to Westward TV programmes on job hunting and unemployment, unemployed young people were encouraged to send for 'Jobhunter kits' and to receive individual or group counselling from adults who formed a network of voluntary helpers and counsellor coordinators. The adult helpers involved in 'Just the Job' had a clear mandate to seek out those unemployed young people who had requested help, by home visits and informal meetings, and to offer personal support and practical help in job finding. The overall aim was to provide positive discrimination to a group which had so far not been given a chance to work, primarily because of their lack of experience and qualifications and the poor local labour market.

Such was the overall success of 'Just the Job' that the project was transported to London by the National Extension College to form the basis of Capital Radio Jobmate in May 1979. This time, however, local radio rather than television was the main medium used for publicizing the project. The first task of the coordinating team was to set up a community-based network of volunteer helpers called Jobmates. With their own employment experience and contacts and knowledge of the local community, they were seen as the key resource to offer the young unemployed. The aims of the project were to:

1 to support young people during unemployment by boosting their morale and confidence;
2 to encourage them to make more effective use of their time whilst unemployed;
3 to improve their skill at looking for jobs and handling interviews;
4 to help them make more regular and constructive use of job-finding and other agencies;
5 to support them during their early days of working life.

In practice, the young people who responded to the radio broadcasts were invited to send for a Jobmate kit and asked if they wanted to talk to one of the Jobmates in the project. A Jobmate handbook was also produced for the Jobmates taking part, based on the handbook used for the 'Just the Job' project (Dauncey, 1978).

The results of Capital Jobmate are impressive, both in terms of the numbers of young people who have rquested help and in the success of the Jobmates themselves (see Table 6.2). Much of this success is clearly attributable to the energy and resourcefulness of the generalist helpers — the Jobmates — and to the intensive individual support that was given to those unemployed who sought help. The coordinating team is quick to point out that whereas each Careers Officer has a caseload of 300 or 400 clients, Jobmates will help between seven and ten unemployed youngsters a year.

The following statistics show some of the groups assisted by the project:

70 per cent of those young people helped had few or no qualifications;
55 per cent were female;
45 per cent were of ethnic minority origin;
41 per cent were not in receipt of benefit.

Table 6.2.   *The Number of People Helped by Capital Jobmate*

	Kits sent to young people	Requests for a Jobmate	Young people helped by a Jobmate
22.10.79–Dec.79	2,600	1,100	500
Jan.80–Dec.80	9,400	2,100	1,400
Jan.81–Dec.81	11,400	3,000	1,600
Jan.82–Dec.82	13,500	3,200	1,800
	36,900	9,400	5,300

Reproduced by permission of the Project Coordinator.

The Capital Jobmate project was monitored and researched for the first three years of its operation and some of the evaluation data is given below.

During the first three years of the project 65.5% of young people put in touch with a Jobmate had moved into work, further education or training. The project's fourth year, 1982, was a bleak year for youth unemployment: and it was expected to be a bleak year for Jobmate. But of those put in touch with a Jobmate, 70.3 per cent moved into work, further education or training, as shown below:

	Percentages
Work	46.2
Youth Opportunities Programme	12.2
Training Opportunities Programme	1.9
Other MSC scheme	2.0
Further education	8.0
	70.3

The project has also had implications for the Jobmates — the volunteer helpers — taking part. By helping young people and taking part in counselling training offered by the project, Jobmates will inevitably develop their own skills of counselling and supporting other people. The very process of helping young people identify their skills, abilities and become effective in job search may also be a potent learning experience for the trainer/consultant. As one former Jobmate put it, 'It increased my self-confidence and made me more tolerant. I learned a lot, for example, about prejudice over issues to do with colour and sexuality. It also made me more aware of the unemployment situation and why it existed.' Participation in the project, it seems, was instrumental in developing personal skills and effecting attitude change.

The Brighton Pre-Employment Project

Innovation in education carries with it a unique set of problems and calls for particular strategies and competencies on the part of the innovator. Trying to innovate across institutional boundaries, particularly those concerned with schooling, employment and training, is a yet more difficult process. The Brighton Pre-Employment Project is an example of one such innovation. Its aim is to provide pupils of low academic ability with a chance to take part in structured work experience and skill sampling courses in the last three terms at school. Its rationale was, therefore, in part compensatory — it was an attempt to upgrade the employment chances of this group of pupils in what was proving to be an increasingly competitive job market. In part it was also supplementary, in providing an additional, perhaps more relevant focus, for the final year of compulsory schooling for pupils who were likely to leave without any formal qualification. The coordinator of the project, having herself worked in a special school and being used to running integrated leavers' programmes, felt that the experience of special education could be used to good effect with pupils in 'normal' comprehensive schools.

The project has been concerned, unashamedly, with vocational preparation — skill sampling courses — across a range of work settings backed up by school-based careers education concerned primarily with developing communication skills. Each term all pupils attended one-day courses at technical colleges or in industrial and work settings; this is reinforced by three separate weeks of related work experience. The courses include Electrical Installation, Motor Vehicle Maintenance, Building, Horticulture and Domestic Services. In 1983 the Project commenced its fifth year of operation, involving 230 pupils from eleven schools in the Brighton area, with teaching staff responsible for recommending and selecting pupils. Entry to the project is therefore limited to students who are likely to derive most benefit.

As in other community-based projects, some of the most notable features concern the cross-fertilization of ideas amongst participants and the links made amongst people who ordinarily would never come into contact. In this particular case, employers from some of the 150 employing organizations taking part have been invited to make contributions to the quality of school-based classroom work. Teachers have been encouraged to visit and supervise pupils whilst on their out-of-school placements.

In-service training days for teachers have been used to develop curriculum materials, and innovation has taken place across the schools taking part. Joint meetings also take place between the teachers involved in the Project and technical college tutors. The Schools Council Communication and Social Skills Project has been involved in curriculum development with the active participation of both teachers and pupils. It is clear that the degree of cooperation and collaboration of individuals drawn from different organizations has provided a successful framework within which the pupils themselves can learn and develop. The project has in effect become a community enterprise.

Assessment and Evaluation

The assessment of the pupils who take part shares many of the characteristics of profiling. Each pupil keeps a record of achievement, attendance and skills learned. School staff, employers and college tutors are invited to assess each pupil's record against an albeit limited range of criteria concerned with punctuality and appearance, as well as skill performance. The certificates presented to those completing the project successfully have, it seems, been effective in securing jobs.

Whilst no formal evaluation of the project has yet taken place, it is clear that an increasing number of schools and pupils wish to join. Most schools taking part have reported improved levels of attainment on the part of pupils involved in the project. The author's analysis of the pupils' own assessment of the Project yields results which are hardly surprising. The young participants are unanimous in wanting to continue with the Project rather than spend their time doing school-based work. Most see the relevance of the Project to their life after school — 'it's teaching me what it's like to go out to work.' For others it is an opportunity for transition learning and to anticipate what their work life will be like, 'I think I have learned to get up earlier and get there on time;' 'It's made me realise that work is not as bad as people say it is.' Others record that their participation in the project has increased their sense of confidence and maturity. 'P.E.P. makes me feel more grown up.' Much of the positive feedback of those taking part seems to result from their perception of the relevance of skill learning and vocational preparation to their own futures. 'I have learned skills that will help me in time to come.'

An Integrated Programme for Business Students: Job Study

Conventionally, one of the principal ways that careers officers and careers advisers gain occupational information is to carry out job studies — detailed reports on various kinds of occupation, usually derived from interviews with people at work. Much of the information is then used by the advisers in individual interviews with clients. How much more effective it is, though, to encourage clients to carry out the job study to improve their own job knowledge and opportunity awareness and to learn at first hand! This was the basic rationale behind a careers programme designed for polytechnic business studies students who needed to know more about the ways they could use their qualifications and skills in the employment market.

The programme itself was, over a period of time, successfully integrated into the students' course of study. Courses in business studies validated by the Business Education Council have a component which is designed to be multidisciplinary, involve local issues and develop problem solving skills for the students taking part. This particular kind of assignment which sets out to answer the question, 'what will I do when I complete my course of study?', is the ideal vehicle for a careers education programme and meets fairly successfully the criteria set by BEC of involving students in analyzing real business situations, by using tasks which are relevant to the level of students' actual or likely work experience, and which do not originate from the perspective of one particular subject discipline. The broad aim, therefore, was to integrate a careers education programme, which had the self and opportunity awareness and decision and transition learning objectives mentioned earlier, within a business studies higher diploma course:

1   to enable students on the course to identify ways of using their interests, skills and the BEC Higher National Diploma in Business Studies in work settings;
2   to place all students in direct contact with people at work and employing organizations, in fields which the students select on the basis of their job and career aspirations;
3   to provide an information resource for all members of the course, by pooling the results of their individual research.

To achieve these objectives in a short programme was obviously expecting a lot from those taking part — an issue covered under the evaluatory note which follows. However, during the week's programme, students were given introductory sessions on the aim of the programme and after input sessions on how to interview people at work, each student was asked to decide on a particular job that they would like to study in depth, arrange an appointment with a person undertaking that kind of work, and after carrying out an extended 'Job Study' interview asked to write a 'Job Study' report. In carrying out the task, they were asked to pay as much attention to the process as they were to the content material. In other words, they were asked to state a rationale for their choice of interviewee, comment on the way they approached the interview procedure and evaluate, for themselves, the interview and their own learning. Supplementary sessions during the week included former students talking about their work, as well as sessions on job search skills and a focus on the employment market for those with business studies qualifications. Group seminar sessions were scheduled to help students define their subject for the 'Job Study' and to give them the chance for a preliminary report back prior to the submission of their individual assignment. In its methodology, this particular study relied heavily on as many implicit careers education objectives as it did on explicit ones. For example, in framing a decision about the kind of interview to undertake, students were *de facto* making a statement about their own aspirations and level of occupational awareness. By leaving the institution to negotiate interviews, they were both exploring the local employment infrastructure and improving their self-presentation skills. By discussing in groups their plans and their findings, they were improving the chances of mutual support and providing the opportunity for peer counselling. The week's programme, it seemed, provided an opportunity for many different kinds of learning.

Results and Evaluation

Over 150 students have taken part in the programme during the last three years. All have managed to complete the task, although some experienced a degree of anxiety in approaching individuals and organizations. Tutors reported that in seminar sessions students found it easy to share perceptions about work and the employment market, as well as about themselves in relation to work.

In finding people to interview, the students relied heavily on the principle of networking; they approached former acquaintances, family friends, contacts of their department and of the careers counselling unit. Some actively sought out former students from their own course. Others used the polytechnic's own resources and interviewed appropriate polytechnic staff.

In the final analysis, the programme depended for its success on the energy and enterprise of the students taking part, as well as the goodwill of the working people they chose as interviewees. Students were surprised at the generosity of the people they interviewed in giving up their time and of the spirit of cooperation they found. Many were entertained and bought lunch. Some were offered full- or part-time work. They gained advice and feedback about their career plans and the relevance of their qualifications to business settings. They learned how to interview, how to approach employers, how to use contacts, how to analyze a particular job and the tasks involved in different occupations. They also discovered something about the range of different sources of guidance and support.

However, there remained the problem of how to determine whether the careers education objectives of self-awareness, transition learning and decision readiness had been achieved. Of these three sets of objectives, primary attention was paid to decision readiness. A modified version of Daws' (1975) Occupational Crystallization self-appraisal questionnaire was used before and after the week's programme to see if students had a more certain idea of their career objectives and the kind of work they might do when their course was completed. The results of this analysis, while not statistically significant, did show that students had, as a group, moved towards more positive decision statements after the week's programme, suggesting that the week had been instrumental in consolidating ideas about their future career plans.

The four case studies described in this chapter provide examples of projects and programmes which exist for the most part outside the work of the formal guidance agencies and have been motivated in response to an identifiable need — in the case of Jobmate and TWL, that of the young unemployed. It could be argued that, in future, community-based projects could form the basis of many new initiatives in the careers guidance field. It will be interesting to see, for example, whether guidance for YTS trainees becomes a coordinated task, under-taken by tutors, supervisors, trainees and careers specialists alike, or whether it operates on a piecemeal and fragmentary basis. To some extent this will clearly depend on the way the formal guidance agencies, in particular the local authority Careers Services, take responsibility for coordinating and integrating guidance activities with the wider community. American experience suggests that careers guidance will become an activity which will be firmly integrated with the wider community and not just be a task for the careers specialist.

The Integrated Community Guidance Programme

In an analysis of American programmes concerned with the preparation for adult and working life, Law (1982) attempts to show how integrated community programmes can help young people with the school to work transition. Integration in this sense is help that comes from a wider range of resources in the school or community, which is coordinated in a way which enables all elements to be visible, in which cross-fertilization takes place within the network of contacts and, finally, in which the network itself and its resources become directly accessible to school students and young people themselves.

Law cites examples of a number of American projects, often community-based, which meet the criteria for integration described above. Projects are by and large organized across institutional boundaries and are designed to give students immediate 'hands on' experience of a range of activities similar to those found in British work experience schemes. Students help run a riding school, prepare exhibitions in a museum or work with artists and craftsmen in their studios, rather than listen to careers talks or watch TV careers programmes. Centrally administered by project coordinators and councils or monitoring groups, they invite participation from students from all schools and colleges in a particular community. In this form of experience-based careers education, students from schools all over the United States are spending up to one day a week in programmes which take them out of school settings, but all of which have the common aim that of teaching something that will be helpful in their future career development.

The results of this integrated approach to community guidance for those taking part appear to be several. Firstly, students are provided with adult role models and learn to relate to adults in the community. Secondly, they find support and encouragement for their plans and aspirations by sharing ideas with peers and other members of the community. At the same time they get feedback about themselves in terms of skills and competencies, particularly as a result of experience-based learning. A further feature — and perhaps the most important from the careers point of view — is that students and school leavers are likely to be able to identify opportunities for work and for leisure. By making contacts, they will hear of vacancies, of work that's available, of training courses that exist in their area. As in the Grubb Institute TWL programme and Capital Radio's Jobmate, the network of personal contacts and resource people increases the life chances of the client group, whether recent school leavers or long-term unemployed.

It remains to be seen whether the American experience will

influence British initiatives and developments in the field of community-based guidance programmes. Certainly, the evidence from the British case studies described earlier in this chapter is that there are tangible gains for young people who participate in programmes of this kind and gains, too, for the resource people and organizations who take part and form part of local networks.

If institutional boundaries of schools, in particular, can be transcended and if the professional groups — teachers and careers advisers — who will be most directly affected by such programmes do not become defensively territorial, more imaginative programmes will be developed to help students and young adults with the transition from school to what lies beyond. The one agency familiar with a coordinating role and ideally placed for this kind of networking operation is, of course, the local authority Careers Service.

Chapter 7

Resources for Careers Counselling and Careers Education

Many of the materials used in careers education and counselling are 'home produced'. Careers practitioners, rightly, devise their own checklists, questionnaires and classroom materials for use with a particular client group, perhaps adapting published materials for use with their own student groups. Any list of careers education materials is therefore unlikely to be entirely comprehensive and will be unable to represent what is being practised under the name of 'careers'.

The aim of this compilation of resources for careers education and counselling is simply to give an idea of the range of published materials available. It is by no means exhaustive, but gives some examples which relate to certain topic headings, such as Decision Making. For the most part, I have concentrated on those published materials which are currently available and which serve either as an aid to individual careers counselling sessions or as material for group and classroom use. To this extent, most of the materials listed are concerned with careers as a process of learning and development rather than the limited definition of 'getting a job'. General occupational information in book, information sheet, audio visual and catalogue forms has been excluded, since several digests already exist on the range and nature of careers and occupational information. The material can often be adapted to suit any age group. *Exercises in Personal and Career Development*, for example, is used as a source book by careers teachers for fourth year students and by careers advisers and counsellors in higher education! Many of the careers education exercises will therefore be applicable to a number of educational settings.

Resource Books for Careers Practitioners

Practical Approaches to Careers Education
C. Avent, CRAC, 1976

A handbook of resources and suggestions for careers education in the classroom and organizing a guidance department.

Practical Aspects of Guidance 1 and 2
David Cleaton and Rob Foster, Careers Consultants, 1981/82

The first of a series of booklets on careers work in schools. The first is concerned with how to mount a careers education programme relevant to the successive year points, and the second is concerned with the organization of school guidance programmes and includes some useful self-training exercises.

Coventry Workscape — A Local Collection of Resource Materials for Schools
Edited by Edwin Langdale, President Kennedy School, Coventry, 1982

Designed for careers practitioners in Coventry with details of every aspect of the local opportunity structure, it includes notes on the local economic, occupational levels and entry points and training in FE and HE.

Starting Points
Gerald March, Gerald March Publishing, 1981

A guide to planning and implementing careers education, it reviews a range of published materials and assesses them against a range of careers education topics.

Careers Education (General)

Work, Parts I, II and III
Schools Council, Longmans, 1978, 1979

A comprehensive set of teaching materials for careers education for use with all ability groups (13–16). Looks at 'careers' from a broad perspective and covers life style and the trade-off between self and work. Each magazine workbook covers a different theme and is supported by a teachers' manual. Relies heavily on participative methods: group discussion and projects. Designed by the Schools Council Careers Education and Guidance Project.

Work It Out
T. Barber, R. Lancashire, J. Steward and P. White, CRAC/Inner London Education Authority Materials Learning Service, 1977

A fifth year programme (materials and audio tape) on self-assessment, fitting people to jobs, analyzing advertisements, designed for leavers with one or two O-levels or CSEs.

Exercises in Personal and Career Development
Barrie Hopson and Patricia Hough, CRAC, 1973

In many ways a forerunner to 'Lifeskills'. The book contains a series of exercises concerned with developing self-awareness, decision-making, values, life style and life planning. It also serves as an introductory text on the concept of career development.

Exercises in Careers Education and Further Exercises in Careers Education
David Cleaton, Careers Consultants, 1976, 1977

A set of classroom careers education exercises for all ability groups, ages 13–16. Topics include self-assessment, finance, opportunities and decision-making.

The Staras Leavers' Programme
Remedial Supply Company, Dixon Street, Wolverhampton

Set of work sheets for slow learners and those in remedial groups to do with work, money, the home, shopping, etc.

Bulls Eye Series
Tony Crowley and Althea Braithwaite, CRAC/Hobsons, 1982

A series of four books on choosing, finding, starting and keeping a job, designed for the average and below ability school leaver in the transition from school to work.

Lift Off from School
Peter March and Tony Western, 1973

Considers career choice, self-assessment, job applications and interviews. A workbook for fourth and fifth years.

Computer-Based Guidance Systems

Cascaid
Cascaid Unit, West Annex, County Hall, Glenfield, Leicester

Designed originally as a guidance aid for Careers Officers in their work with secondary school students, Cascaid is now also available for students in higher education. As with the other main systems in use, it matches a student's profile against a bank of job titles to provide suitable occupational suggestions.

Job Ideas and Information Generator Computer Assisted Learning (JIIG/CAL)
Dr S.J. Closs, Department of Business Studies, Edinburgh University, William Robertson Building, George Square, Edinburgh EH8 9JY

Computer-based careers education and guidance system for young people and adults. Provides occupational suggestions and further information to suit students' interests. Used by careers officers and careers teachers, it can be used as the basis for individual careers counselling or careers education in schools.

Gradscope
Dr L. Wilson, Central Services Unit, Crawford House, Precinct Centre, Oxford Road, Manchester M13 9EP

A computer-based system which offers suitable occupational suggestions to users, who are usually graduates and students from more vocationally oriented degree subjects. Used largely as a basis for individual counselling.

MAUD (Multi Attribute Utility Decomposition)
SELSTRA (Self Elaborated Structuring and Assessment)
Stuart Wooler, Decision Analysis Unit, London School of Economics and Political Science

Two problems which have been designed to facilitate the career decision-making process, by looking at the way clients structure their decisions (see Chapter 5).

Deciding/Decision-Making

Deciding
A.G. Watts and D. Elsom, CRAC, 1974

A set of decision-making exercises for classroom use, adapted from an American programme designed for teaching decision-making skills. Looks at decision-making styles and strategies.

Decide for Yourself
Bill Law, CRAC/Hobsons, 1977

A workbook on career decision-making which can be used on an individual basis or as a framework for classroom use. Sections on assessing values, abilities and personal styles. Useful for any age of student.

Educational Choices

Your Choice at 13+
V. Mathew and M. Smith, CRAC, 1972

A guide for students third year choice of subject options, it looks at the implications of O-level and CSE subjects for future career choice.

Your Choice at 17+: Your Choice at 15+
P. March and M. Smith, CRAC, 1977

Part of a series of handbooks on educational and occupational choices. In part fact giving, in part self-help material, both look at the range of options available at each stage, and detail the range of types of training, jobs and further study available.

Interests

Pictorial Interests Guide
Tony Crowley, CRAC, 1974

A set of picture cards, each colour coded, to be used as a basis for occupational grouping which is designed to elicit occupational preferences and choices. Particularly designed for ESN and less able groups.

Occupational Checklist
Tony Crowley, CRAC, 1976

A simple interests questionnaire which can be used as a basis for individual counselling. Particularly relevant to sixth form groups and A-level students.

Occupational Interests Blank
Tony Crowley, CRAC, 1976

An interest guide for average ability third and fourth year groups (see Chapter 4).

Job Retention and Adjustment

Starting Work
Basic Skills Unit, COIC, 1981

A series of five exercises with a magazine, concerned with the social skills that are important at the work place.

The School Leavers' Book
B. Cannings, Longman Group, 1983

A cartoon-based book on workers' rights, statutory benefits and welfare issues designed by the students and staff of the Small Heath School and Community Centre.

Job Search, Applications and Interviews

Working in a City
Edited by Seline Hassell and Cathy Charlton, FEH Curriculum Development Project, Inner London Education Authority, 1978

Extensive set of curriculum materials covering the themes of deciding, finding and applying, interviewing and work and money. Particularly useful checklist for simulating and observing selection interviews. Designed largely for young people in London.

Ways to Work
Colin and Mog Ball, COIC, 1982

An illustrated workbook which looks briefly at self-assessment, classifying jobs and sources of information.

Ambush
Fional Wilson, CRAC, 1982

Simple snakes and ladders game based on Do's and Don'ts of Job Hunting which can be played by up to six players at a time.

Jobkit
Basic Skills Unit and the Manpower Services Commission, written by Joanna Fawkes, 1983

This is a basic pack of self-help materials on job search and related topics sent to enquirers as part of the Capital Radio Jobmate Project.

Game for a Job
COIC, 1982

A twenty-five-minute video which uses the context of an imaginary quiz show to look at the process of job search. It covers four separate stages: the letter, the 'phone call, the application form and the interview.

Life Skills Teaching

Lifeskills Teaching Programme No. 1 and No. 2
Barrie Hopson, Mike Scally, Lifeskills Associates, Leeds, 1982

There are over a hundred exercises in these two volumes which are designed to be used in a variety of contexts, with a wide range of client groups. Each exercise has a clearly defined life skills objective, for example, 'to help students identify their primary learning style', and each is provided with a detailed set of instructions and resource notes. The topics range from those concerned with interpersonal skills, for example, how to be assertive and how to communicate effectively, to those concerned with study, for example, how to study effectively and time management, to those concerned with work and how to find a job and how to cope with unemployment. As well as the exercises themselves, detailed notes are provided about classroom management and facilitating group discussion. It provides a comprehensive teaching programme, particularly appropriate for all careers practitioners, counsellors, tutors and youth workers.

Skills for Life
Lesley Kaye-Beasley and Dilwyn Byles, Stanley Thornes Ltd. 1979

A comprehensive series of practical life skills exercises with personal budgeting, law, social security, becoming a worker and social issues, such as prejudice, the role of women and violence. Much of it takes the form of questionnaire checklists, such as 'How old do you have to be to open a bank account?', and the right answers are all provided.

Life Skills Training Manual
Published by Community Service Volunteers, 237 Pentonville Road, London N1, 1973

A manual for life skills trainers with a wealth of different exercises, simulations, and background materials covering five different life styles: leisure, job, personal, family, and community.

Learning from Experience in Working Life
The Resource Book for Teachers in F.E. and Industry, The Rubber Products and Plastics Industry Training Board, 1982

A handbook for tutors involved in UVP and life and social skills, which is a large compilation of exercises, many with an industrial flavour.

Life after School — A Social Skills Curriculum
James McGuire and Philip Priestley, Pergamon, 1981

A social and life skills manual which provides a theoretical context, examples of programmes materials and curriculum implications. Topics include self-assessment, communications, job search, leisure, working and legal rights.

Basic Skills You Need
H.M. Dobinson, Nelson, 1976

A book of simple classroom topics and exercises ranging from form filling and letter writing to using timetables and telephones.

Teaching Social and Life Skills
John Blyth, Diane Brace, Tony Henry, National Extension College, 1979

This is not a teaching package, but a handbook on how to implement social and life skills. It details key learning objectives for each life skill and looks at the specific and general needs of trainees.

Matching Systems

Computajob and *Advanced Computajob*
Tony Crowley, CRAC, 1972

Student questionnaires concerned with abilities and conditions of work are matched against 150 job titles to give individual students some job suggestions. Available also as microcomputer programme.

Job Match
Macmillan Educational, Basingstoke, written by the Staff of the Industrial Training Research Unit, 1982

This is a self-assessment package for use in individual counselling with average ability school leavers. Questionnaires about social and work involvement, work content, etc. are matched against forty job titles. An interactive computer version is also available.

Occupational Awareness

Speedcop
Charlotte Hopson, Barrie Hopson and John Hayes, CRAC, 1973

A board game for two to six students looking at occupations against a framework of eight different job features: surroundings, prospects, entry and training, effects, description of work conditions, organization and people.

Close-up Packs
COIC

Film strips, tape slides and overhead transparencies on work in different industrial sectors, such as construction, engineering, distribution, focusing on jobs and work with some additional careers education exercises and role play materials.

Job Knowledge Indices
Michael Kirton, COIC and Heinemann Educational, 1979

A series of questionnaires and answer sheets aimed at testing students' occupational knowledge. Designed for above average ability groups and relevant in the main to the 16–18 age group. Can be used for individual or group work.

Redundancy

Redundancy Pack
Published by the Redundancy Pack Team, Nelson and Colne College, Nelson, Lancashire, 1982

A folder of notes designed for people who have been made redundant in mid-career, which covers topics like organizing one's finances, claiming benefit and finding work.

Self-Help Materials

Working It Out
Careers and Occupational Information Centre, 1982

A workbook and self-help manual designed primarily for adults in mid-career. It looks at the factors involved in job choice and career development, with a particular emphasis on career decision-making.

Making a Living
Ruth Silver, Inner London Education Authority, 1979

A self-help pack designed for use with low/average ability groups which can be used in individual and group settings.

Career Change
Ruth Lancashire and Roger Holdsworth, CRAC, 1976.

Designed principally for adults in mid-career, the book contains a number of exercises concerned with career and life planning, self-assessment and decision-making. A final chapter deals with implementing ideas and job search.

Routes 1
Tim Kemp, CRAC, 1982

A workbook which is based on cartoons, designed for statutory age leavers which is concerned with options after the fifth year.

What Colour Is Your Parachute? — A Practical Manual for Job Hunters and Career Changers
Richard Nelson Bolles, Ten Speed Press, Berkeley Ca., 1972

More than a simple guide to writing a curriculum vitae or locating likely employers, this deals as much with the psychological issues to do with job search, (rejection, shock, decision-making, etc.) as with the practical issues of preparing for interviews. In many ways the complete 'self-help' manual for career changers, it unashamedly encourages a proactive, self-managing approach to job hunting and has written into its exercises and text the exhortation to 'identify the person who has the power to hire you and show them how your skills can help them with their problems'. Its one drawback is that the text still assumes that work equals full-time paid employment and omits themes such as how to create alternatives to work as we know it.

The Three Boxes of Life and How to Get out of Them
Richard Nelson Bolles, Ten Speed Press, Berkeley, Ca., 1978

This is a guide to life and career planning. Written for American students and mid-career changers, it uses extensive examples of the United States job market and economy and may, therefore, not be easy to use in UK guidance settings. It is, however, an immensely valuable source book of exercises and examples which can be used for careers education or career/life planning programmes. It addresses the individual with questions about the three boxes of life: Learning, Work and Play. Particularly suitable for 18+ age group and for adults facing mid-career review. Like 'Parachute', however, it tends to equate work with full-time paid employment.

Unemployment

Working It Out — Don't Let Them Waste Your Time and *The Survival Game*
Community Services Volunteers, 237 Pentonville Rd., London N1, 1983.

Values Clarification

Work Shuffle — A Teaching Programme for Discovering Work Values
Barrie Hopson and Mike Scally, Lifeskills Associates, Leeds, 1982

A set of eight exercises which are designed to help clients broaden their understanding of the nature of work identity, their work values and how these values relate to various kinds of work, both paid and unpaid.

Suitable for group work with clients of all ages, the programme uses a card sort as the basis for most of the exercises, with different cards representing different value statements.

Meeting Yourself Halfway
S.B. Simon, Argus, 1974

A handbook on values clarification, and a standard American text.

Work

Starting Work
The Industrial Society, 1972

A simple film strip and tape commentary on the nature and organization of work, the role of unions and management, etc.

It's Your Future
National Extension College in conjunction with Thames Television, 1978

A series of ten work sheets in magazine style to back up a series of television programmes on the nature of work and unemployment, etc.

Male and Female
A. Jones, J. Marsh and A.G. Watts (CRAC), 1974

A classroom workbook on the theme of changing sex roles in relation to work, part of a series which also looks at life style and leisure.

Touch Down to Work
Peter March and Tony Western, 1973 CRAC

Classroom workbooks for fourth and fifth year students of average ability. Looks at the implications of work and the impact of work on life style.

Work Experience

Work Experience Books
Alan Jameson, CRAC/Hobsons 1981

Teachers' handbook and student workbook designed to make the best of work experience programmes by preparation and structured observation.

Work Experience
Edited by Seline Hassell and Jane Harrison, Inner London Education Authority Publishing Centre, Highbury Station Road, London N1 1SB, 1980

Comprehensive workpack designed for 15–19-year-olds who are on further education courses with a work experience element which could equally be used in schools. The aim is to make work experience a period of structured learning, and it includes separate work sheets and recommended reading lists on different commercial and industrial sectors.

Appendix 1

Organizations Concerned with Training

Careers Research Advisory Centre,
Bateman Street, Cambridge, CB2 1LZ

Counselling and Career Development Unit,
Leeds University, Leeds, LS2 9JT

Local Government Training Board,
4th Floor, Arndale House, Arndale Centre, Luton, LU1 2TS

National Institute for Careers Education and Counselling,
Bayfordbury House, Lower Hatfield Road, Hertford, SG13 8LD

Appendix 2

Professional Organizations

Association of Graduate Careers Advisory Services,
The Secretary,
The University of Leeds,
Careers Service,
Leeds LS2 9JT

British Association of Counselling,
la Little Church Street,
Rugby,
Warwicks CV21 3AP

Institute of Careers Officers,
The General Secretary,
2nd Floor, Old Board Chambers,
37A High Street,
Stourbridge DY8 ITA

National Association of Careers and Guidance Teachers,
General Secretary,
9 Lawrence Leys,
Bloxham,
Banbury,
Oxon OX15 4NU

Bibliography

ADAMS, J., *et al.* (1976) *Transition: Understanding and Managing Personal Change*, London, Martin Robertson.

ANASTASI, A. (1976) *Psychological Testing*, London, Collier Macmillan.

ARMSTRONG, D., *et al.* (1981) *TWL Network in Practice — Supporting Young People in Transition to Working Life*, Grubb Institute.

ARROBA, T. (1977) 'Styles of decision making and their use: An empirical study', *British Journal of Guidance and Counselling*, 5, 2.

ASHTON, D.N. and FIELD, D. (1976) *Young Workers*, London, Hutchinson.

ASHTON, D.N. and McGUIRE, M.J. (1980) 'The Careers Service and the local labour market', *Careers Bulletin*, Summer.

ASPECTS OF SECONDARY EDUCATION IN ENGLAND (1979) HMI Report, London, HMSO.

BALDWIN, J. and WELLS, H. (1980) *Active Tutorial Work*, Basil Blackwell.

BAZALGETTE, J. (1978) *School Life and Work Life*, London, Hutchinson.

BEDFORD, T. (1982a) *Vocational Guidance Interviews*, Department of Employment Careers Service Branch, July.

BEDFORD, T. (1982b) *Vocational Guidance Interviews Explored: A Model and Some Training Implications*, Department of Employment Careers Service Branch, December.

BENJAMIN, A. (1969) *The Helping Interview*, Boston, Mass., Houghton Mifflin.

BEST, R., *et al.* (1980) *Perspectives on Pastoral Care*, London, Heinemann.

BLACK, D. (1976) 'Work experience: A systematic approach', *British Journal of Guidance and Counselling*, 4, 1., pp. 88–97.

BLAU, P.M., *et al.* (1956) 'Occupational choice: A conceptual framework', *Industrial and Labor Relations Review*, 9, 4.

BOX, S. and FORD, J. (1967) 'Sociological theory and occupational choice', *Sociological Review*, 15, 3.

BRAMMER, M. (1979) *The Helping Relationship*, Englewood Cliffs, N.J., Prentice Hall.

BRANNEN, P. (Ed.) (1975) *Entering the World of Work: Some Sociological Perspectives*, London, HMSO.

CARTER, M.P. (1972) *Home, School and Work*, Oxford, Pergamon Press.

CHERRY, N. (1974) 'Do Careers Officers give good advice?', *British Journal of Guidance and Counselling*, 2, pp. 27–40.

CHERRY, N. (1975) 'Occupational values and employment: A follow-up study of graduate men and women', *Higher Education*, 4, pp. 356–68.

CLARKE, L. (1980a) *The Transition from School to Work: A Critical Review of Research in the United Kingdom*, Department of Employment Careers Service Branch, research report.

CLARKE, L. (1980b) *Occupational Choice*, Department of Employment Careers Service Branch, report.

CLARKE, L. (1980c) *The Practice of Vocational Guidance: A Critical Review of Research in the United Kingdom*, Department of Employment Careers Service Branch, research report.

CLOSS, S.J. (1975) *Manual of the APU Guide*, London, Hodder and Stoughton.

CLOSS, S.J. (1980, 1983) *Release I and III*, JIIG-CAL Information Booklets.

COLLINS, T. (1982) *Computers: A View from the Careers Service*, NACGT Guide.

COOLBEAR, J. and FAIRBAIRNS, J. (1981) *Evaluation Study of an Experimental Career Counselling Programme for PER Registrants*, Psychological Services, Manpower Services Commission Training Services Division, Report DTP 23, June.

CRITES, J.O. (1974) 'Career counselling: A review of major approaches', *The Counselling Psychologist*, 4, pp. 3–23.

CRITES, J.O. (1981) *Careers Counselling: Models, Methods and Materials*, McGraw Hill.

CROWLEY, T. (1972) *Technical Data for the Crowley Occupational Interests Blank*, Occasional Paper 2, CRAC.

DAUNCEY, G. (1978) *A Counsellor's Handbook*, 'Just The Job' Project.

DAWS, P.P. (1968) *A Good Start in Life*, Cambridge, Hobsons Press.

DAWS, P. (1975) 'The Keele Occupational Crystallisation Self Appraisal Form', *British Journal of Guidance and Counselling*, 3, 1.

DAWS, P.P. (1976) *Early Days*, Cambridge, Hobsons Press.

DAWS, P.P. (1977) 'Are careers education programmes in secondary schools a waste of time? — A reply to Roberts', *British Journal of Guidance and Counselling*, 5, 1.

DAWS, P.P. (1981) 'The socialisation/opportunity-structure theory of the occupational location of school leavers: A critical appraisal', Chapter 7 in Watts, A.G. *et al*, *Career Development in Britain — Some Contributions to Theory and Practice*, (CRAC) Hobsons Press.

DEPARTMENT OF EDUCATION AND SCIENCE, (1973) *Careers Education in Secondary Schools*, Education Survey 18, London, HMSO.

DEPARTMENT OF EDUCATION AND SCIENCE, (1979) *Aspects of Secondary Education*, London, HMSO.

DEPARTMENT OF EMPLOYMENT, *The Careers Service 1980–1981*, Careers Service Branch.

DEPARTMENT OF EDUCATION AND SCIENCE (1981) *Schools and Working Life:*

Some Initiatives, London, H.M.S.O.

DEVINE, K. (1981) in WHEELOCK, V. *Careers in an Information Society*, University of Bradford.

DOUGLAS, J.W. (1971) *Young School Leavers at Work and College*, unpublished research report from the National Survey, May.

EGAN, G. (1975) *The Skilled Helper: A Model for Systematic Helping and Interpersonal Relating*, Monterey, Ca., Brooks/Cole.

EGGLESTON, J. (Ed.) (1982) *Work Experience in Secondary Schools*, London, Routledge and Kegan Paul.

ENTWISTLE, N. and WILSON, J. (1977) *Degrees of Excellence*, London, Hodder and Stoughton.

FOGELMAN, K. (1979) 'Educational and Career Aspirations of Sixteen-year-olds', *British Journal of Guidance and Counselling*, 7, 1.

GELATT, H.B. (1962) 'Decision Making: A conceptual framework for counselling', *Journal of Counselling Psychology*, 9.

GILMORE, S.K. (1973) *The Counsellor in Training*, Englewood Cliffs, N.J., Prentice-Hall.

GINZBERG, E. (1972) 'Toward a theory of occupational choice: A restatement', *Vocational Guidance Quarterly*, 20, 3.

GINZBERG, E., *et al.* (1951) *Occupational Choice*, New York, Columbia University Press.

GOLDMAN, L. (1971) *Using Tests in Counseling*, 2nd ed., New York, Appleton-Century-Crofts.

GREGORY, D. and REES, T.L. (1978) *Work Experience — A Case Study from South Wales*, Manpower Services Commission, Special Programmes Division.

HALL, D.T. (1976) *Careers in Organisations*, California, Pacific Palisades.

HANSEN, L.S. (1977) *Counseling and Career (Self) Development of Women in Vocational Guidance and Career Development*, in PETERS, H. (Ed.) New York, Macmillan.

HAYES, J. (1971) *Occupational Perceptions and Occupational Information*. Institute of Careers Officers.

HEALEY, C.C. (1982) *Career Development*, Boston, Mass., Allyn and Bacon.

HOLDSWORTH. R. (undated) *Using Tests in Vocational Guidance*, Icon Series 7, Institute of Careers Officers.

HOLLAND, J.L. (1966) *Psychology of Vocational Choice*, Mass, Waltham Blaidell.

HOLLAND, J.L. (1971) *A Counsellors Guide for the Self Directed Search*, Palo Alto, Calif., Consulting Psychologists Press.

HOLLAND, J.L. (1974a) *The Self Directed Search*, Palo Alto, Ca., Consulting Psychologists Press.

HOLLAND, J.L. (1974b) *Making Vocational Choices — A Theory of Careers*, Englewood Cliffs, N.J., Prentice-Hall.

HOPSON, B. and SCALLY, M. (1981) *Lifeskills Teaching*, Maidenhead, McGraw Hill.

Hoyt, K.B. (1975) 'Careers education: Challenges for counselors', *The Vocational Guidance Quarterly*, 23, June, pp. 303–10.

Hoyt, K.B. *et al.* (1972) *Careers Education: What It Is and How to Do It*, Utah, Olympus Publishing Company.

Isaacson, L.L. (1977) *Careers Information in Counseling and Teaching*, Boston, Mass., Allyn and Bacon.

Jahoda, G. and Chalmers, A.D. (1963) 'The Youth Employment Service: A consumer perspective', *Occupational Psychology*, 37.

Jamieson, I. (1982) 'Learning from Work Experience at 14–16' in *Schools, YOP and the New Training Initiative*, Cambridge, CRAC/Hobsons Press.

Jenkins, C. and Sherman, B. (1979) *The Collapse of Work*, London, Methuen.

Katz, M.R. (1969) 'Learning to make wise decisions', in Scates, A.Y. (Ed.) *Computer Based Vocational Guidance Systems*, Washington, D.C., US Government Publishing Office.

Keil, E.T. (1976) *Becoming a Worker: The Induction of School Leavers into Work in Leicestershire*, Leicestershire Committee for Education and Industry.

Kelly, G.A. (1955) 'The psychology of personal constructs', Vol, 1, *A Theory of Personality*, New York, Norton.

Kelsall, R.K., *et al.* (1972) *Graduates: The Sociology of An Elite*, London, Methuen.

Kidd, J.M. (1981) 'The assessment of career development', Chapter 10 in Watts, A.G. *et al.*, *Career Development in Britain — Some Contributions to Theory and Practice*, (CRAC) Hobsons Press.

Kirton, D. (1983) 'The Impact of Mass Unemployment on Careers Guidance in the Durham Coalfield', in Fiddy, R. (Ed.) *In Place of Work: Policy and Provision for the Young Unemployed*, Lewes, Falmer Press.

Kline, P. (1975) *Psychology of Vocational Guidance*, London, Batsford.

Knasel, E., *et al.* (1982) *The Benefit of Experience*, MSC Research and Development Series, No. 5.

Krumboltz, J. (1977) *A Model for Decision Making — Careers Skills Assessment Programme*, College Entrance Examination Board.

Krumboltz, J. and Baker, R. (1973) 'Behavioural counselling for vocational decisions', in Borow, H. (Ed.) *Career Guidance for a New Age*, Boston, Mass., Houghton Mifflin.

Krumboltz, J. and Thoreson, C. (1976) *Counselling*, New York, Holt, Rinehart and Winston.

Law, B. (1977) 'Introduction to Careers Guidance', National Institute for Careers Education and Counselling Training Module.

Law, B. (1978a) 'The concomitants of system orientation in secondary school counsellors', *British Journal of Guidance and Counselling*, 6, 2.

Law, B. (1978b) 'An integrated approach to secondary school guidance', *The Careers and Guidance Teacher*, Spring.

Law, B. (1981) 'Careers theory: A third dimension?', Chapter 9 in Watts, A.G. *et al.*, *Career Development in Britain — Some Contributions to Theory and Practice*, (CRAC) Hobsons Press.

LAW, B. (1982) *Beyond Schooling: A British Analysis of Integrated Programmes of Preparation for Adult and Working Life in the United States*, National Institute for Careers Education and Counselling.

LAWS, B. and WARD, R. (1981) 'Is career development motivated?', Chapter 3 in WATTS, A.G. et al., *Career Development in Britain — Some Contributions to Theory and Practice*, (CRAC) Hobsons Press.

LAW, B. and WATTS, A.G. (1977) *Schools, Careers and Community*, London, Church Information Office.

LLOYD, F. and WILSON, W. (1980) 'Interviews — the first impressions', in *Careers Bulletin*, Department of Employment Careers Service Branch, Summer.

LOCKE, M. and BLOOMFIELD, J. (1982) *Mapping and Reviewing the Pattern of 16–19 Education*, London, Schools Council Pamphlet, No. 20.

LOUDON, A.M. (1982) 'Careers Service Futures', *Careers Bulletin*, Department of Employment Careers Service Branch, Spring.

McGUIRE, J. and PRIESTLEY, P. (1981) *Life after School: A Social Skills Curriculum*, Oxford, Pergamon Press.

MAIZELS, J. (1970) *Adolescent Needs and the Transition from School to Work*, London, Athlone Press.

MILLER, J. et al. (1983) *Towards a Personal Guidance Base*, London, FEU.

MILNER, P. (1974) *Counselling in Education*, London, Dent.

MUSGRAVE, P.W. (1967) 'Towards a sociological theory of occupational choice', *Sociological Review*, 15, 1.

NEWSOME, A. et al. (1973) *Student Counselling in Practice*, University of London Press.

OSIPOW, S.H. (1973) *Theories of Career Development*, New York, Appleton-Century-Crofts.

PARSONS, D. and HUTT, R. (1981) *The Mobility of Young Graduates*, University of Sussex, Institute of Manpower Studies.

PARSONS, F. (1909) *Choosing a Vocation*, Boston, Mass., Houghton Mifflin.

PRIDDLE, C. (Ed.) (1979) *Register of Careers Education Activities, (ROCEA)*, Association of Graduate Careers Advisory Services.

PUMFREY, P.D. and SCHOFIELD, A. (1982) 'Work experience and the career maturity of fifth-form pupils,' *British Journal of Guidance and Counselling*, 10, 2, July, pp. 167–75.

REED, B.D. (1980) 'Preparing school leavers for working life', *Grubb Institute of Behavioural Studies*, February (xeroxed article).

REED, B., et al. (1982) *Becoming Adult*, a proposition paper on the Grubb Institute's work concerning young people, The Grubb Institute.

REUBENS, B.G. (1977) *Bridges to Work*, London, Martin Robertson.

ROBERTS, K. (1968) 'The entry into employment: An approach towards a general theory', *Sociological Review*, 16.

ROBERTS, K. (1971) *From School to Work: A Study of the Youth Employment Service*, Newton Abbot, David and Charles.

ROBERTS, K. (1977) 'The social conditions, consequences and limitations of careers guidance', *British Journal of Guidance and Counselling*, 5, 1.

ROBERTS, K. (1981) 'The sociology of work entry and occupational choice', Chapter 8 in WATTS, A.G., *et al.*, *Career Development in British — Some Contributions to Theory and Practice*, (CRAC) Hobsons Press.

RODGER, A. (1952) *The Seven Point Plan*, London, National Institute of Industrial Psychology.

ROE, A. (1956) *Psychology of Occupations*, New York, Wiley.

ROE, A. (1957) 'Early Determinants of Vocational Choice', *Journal of Counselling Psychology*, 4, pp. 212–217, Copyright 1957, American Psychological Association.

ROGERS, C.R. (1942) *Counselling and Psychotherapy*, Boston, Mass., Houghton Mifflin.

ROGERS, C.R. (1957) 'The necessary and sufficient conditions of therapeutic personality change', *Journal of Consulting Psychology*, 21, pp. 95–103.

SCHEIN, E.H. (1980) *Organizational Psychology*, Englewood Cliffs, NJ, Prentice-Hall

SCHOOLS COUNCIL (1972) *Careers Education in the 1979s*, London, Evans Methuen, Working Paper 40.

SHOWLER, B. and SINFIELD, A. (1981) *The Workless State — Studies in Unemployment*, Oxford, Robertson.

SOFER, C. (1974) 'Introduction' in WILLIAMS, M., (Ed.) *Occupational Choice*, London, Allen and Unwin.

SPEAKMAN, M.A. (1980) 'Occupational choice and placement', in ENGLAND, G. and SALAMAN, G. (Eds) *The Politics of Work and Occupations*, Open University Press.

STANTON, G.P., *et al.* (1980) *Developing Social and Life Skills*, Further Education Curriculum Review and Development Unit.

SUPER, D.E. (1951) 'Vocational Adjustment: Implementing a Self Concept', *Occupations*, Volume 30.

SUPER, D.E. (1953) 'A theory of vocational development', *American Psychologist*, 8.

SUPER, D.E. (1957) *The Psychology of Careers*, New York, Harper and Row.

SUPER, D.E. (1973) 'The career development inventory', *British Journal of Guidance and Counselling*, 1.

SUPER, D.E. (1974) 'Vocational maturity theory: Towards implementing a psychology of careers in careers education and guidance' in SUPER, D.E. (Ed.), *Measuring Vocational Maturity for Counselling and Evaluation*, Washington, D.C., National Vocational Guidance Association.

SUPER, D.E. (1981) 'Approaches to Occupational Choice and Career Development' in WATTS, A.G. *et al.* (Ed.) *Career Development in Britain*, Cambridge, CRAC/Hobsons Press.

THOMAS, R. and WETHERALL, D. (1974) *Looking Forward to Work*, London, Office of Population Census and Surveys Social Division Report, HMSO.

THORNDIKE, R.K. and HAGEN, E. (1959) *10,000 Careers*, New York, Wiley.

TIEDEMAN, D.V. and O'HARA, R.P. (1963) *Career Development: Choice and Adjustment*, New York, College Entrance Examination Board.

TOLBERT, E.L. (1980) *Counselling for Career Development*, Boston, Mass., Houghton Mifflin.

TYLER, L. (1969) *The Work of the Counsellor*, New York, Appleton-Century-Crofts.

WATTS, A.G. (1977) 'Careers education in higher education: Principles and practice', *British Journal of Guidance and Counselling*, 5, 2.

WATTS, A.G. (Ed.) (1983) *Work Experience in Schools* London, Heinemann.

WATTS, A.G. and FAWCETT, B. (1980) 'Pastoral care and careers education', in BEST, R, *et al.*, *Perspectives in Pastoral Care*, London, Heinemann.

WATTS, A.G. and HERR, E.L. (1975) 'Career(s) education in Britain and the USA: Contrasts and common problems', *British Journal of Guidance and Counselling*, 4, 2.

WATTS, A.G., *et al.* (1981) *Career Development in Britain — Some Contributions to Theory and Practice*, (CRAC) Hobsons Press.

WEINRACH, S.G. (Ed.) (1979) *Career Counseling*, New York, McGraw-Hill.

WILLIAMS, W.M. (Ed.) (1974) *Occupational Choice*, London, Allen and Unwin.

WILLIS, P. (1976) in HAMMERSLEY, M. and WOODS, P. (Eds.) *The Process of Schooling*, London, Routledge and Kegan Paul.

WILLIS, P. (1977) *Learning to Labour: How Working Class Kids Get Working Class Jobs*, Farnborough, Saxon House.

WILSON, L. (1979) *Gradscope:* Background paper, Manchester, Central Services Unit.

WOOLER, S. and LEWIS, B. (1982) 'Computer assisted careers counselling: A new approach', *British Journal of Guidance and Counselling*, 10, pp. 124–34.

Subject Index

For Product Safety Concerns and Information please contact our EU
representative GPSR@taylorandfrancis.com
Taylor & Francis Verlag GmbH, Kaufingerstraße 24, 80331 München, Germany